MURDER
AT 40 BELOW

TRUE CRIME STORIES FROM ALASKA

by Tom Brennan

foreword by Sheila Toomey

illustrations by Brian Sostrom

EPICENTER PRESS
ALASKA BOOK ADVENTURES

Epicenter Press Inc. is a regional press founded in Alaska whose interests include but are not limited to the arts, history, environment, and diverse cultures and lifestyles of Alaska and the Pacific Northwest.

Publisher: Kent Sturgis
Acquisitions Editor: Lael Morgan
Editor: Don Graydon
Cover design: Elizabeth Watson
Text design: Victoria Sturgis Michael
Illustrations & maps: Brian Sostrom
Proofreader: Sherrill Carlson
Printer: Transcontinental Printing

Library of Congress Control Number: 2001094971
ISBN 978-0-945397-99-1

PRINTED IN CANADA
10 9 8 7 6 5

To order single copies of MURDER AT 40 BELOW, mail $14.95 plus $6 for Priority Mail shipping (WA residents add $1.85 state sales tax) to: Epicenter Press, PO Box 82368, Kenmore, WA 98028, phone our toll-free order line at 1-800-950-6663, or order online at www.EpicenterPress.com.

This book is dedicated to the memory of
Trooper Troy Duncan and the Alaska police
officers who put their lives on the line that the
rest of us may live in peace.

CONTENTS

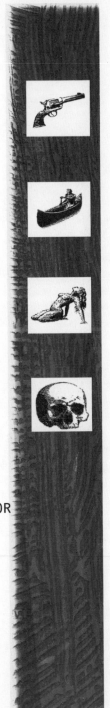

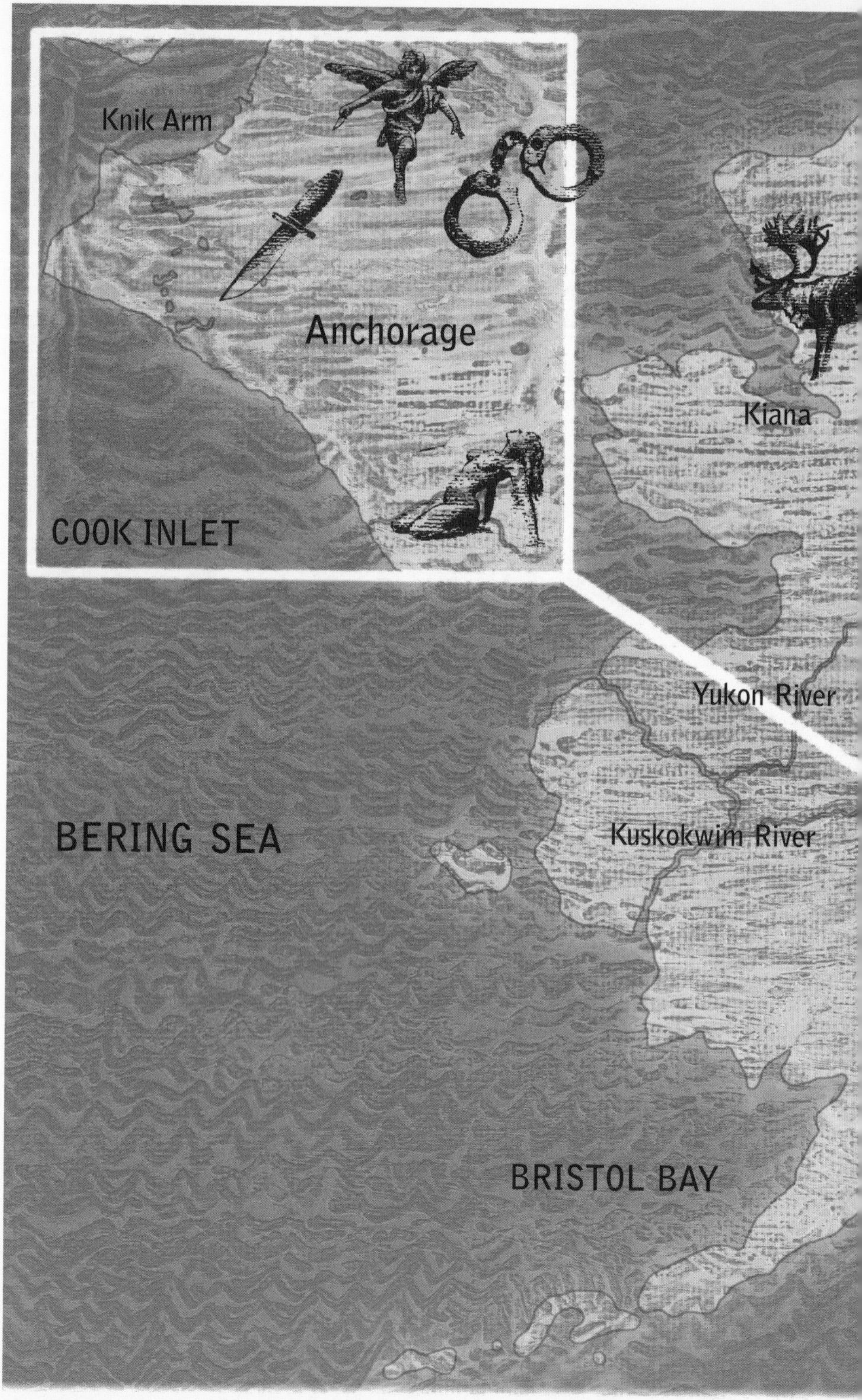

Knik Arm
Anchorage
Kiana
COOK INLET
Yukon River
BERING SEA
Kuskokwim River
BRISTOL BAY

BROOKS RANGE

Manley

Fairbanks

Chulitna

McCarthy

Cordova

Seward

Juneau

GULF OF ALASKA

FOREWORD

Is it just imagination or does murder in Alaska have a special edge, a rawness that suggests the violation of a dream?

Homicide happens everywhere, in big Eastern cities and little Southern towns, on boats off any shore and in cabins at the heart of any forest. But it seems somehow more wrong when it happens in a place Americans think of as their last pristine wilderness. There's a disconnect between what they accept as commonplace in Detroit or Miami or Chicago and what Outsiders want to believe about Alaska.

The truth is, most Alaskans came here from somewhere else and they brought their bad habits with them.

We born-again Alaskans like to put on airs—talk about how tough the weather is here and call ourselves pioneers even though the kind of pioneering that confers bragging rights ended with World War II. The truth is, most of us are ordinary people—good and bad, brave or frightened, successful or not, flawed in the ways we all learn to live with.

Alaskans use a rough code to describe the different kinds of people who have been drawn north to what was until the mid-twentieth century little more than a sparsely settled outpost. There are the tree huggers; the rape-and-ruiners; the new-lifers; and the end-of-the-roaders.

Tree huggers are people seeking escape from cities: outdoor types like mountain climbers and hikers, or serious adventurers who want to relive the pioneer experience, to build a cabin, haul water, smoke fish, live simply. Or they can be people who are simply tired of breathing smog. They come for what we have most of, the outdoors.

Rape-and-ruiners are, in unkind shorthand, those who come north to make money, to mine or construct or drill or sell. During the building of the trans-Alaska pipeline, thousands of these questers flooded into Anchorage each month. They tend to go back where they come from after a few years.

New-lifers are people dissatisfied with the life they made somewhere else. They are looking to start over where there's less competition and more room to take a chance. As a restaurant owner in Nome once told me: "All the big-wheel spokes back home were taken. If you wanted to be somebody, you had to wait for someone to die, and then there were dozens of others looking to take his place."

End-of-the-roaders are a different breed. You will meet a lot of them in Tom Brennan's murder chronicles. These are people who have worn out their welcome everywhere they've been, who have fled or been chased to the edge of the world—as far away from home as they can drive and still be an American.

Sometimes they are fleeing law enforcement, like Kirby Anthoney, who was suspected of raping a teenager in Twin Falls, Idaho, and leaving her for dead. He moved to Anchorage to start over, living for a time with relatives. You'll find out how he repaid his aunt and uncle for their kindness. Robert Hansen, a nerdy baker who liked to hunt and could fly a plane, fled his Midwest criminal history but never lost his taste for hookers. Once in Alaska, he established a successful business, bought a nice home, and started a family. He also murdered at least seventeen women, many of them prostitutes.

Some end-of-the-roaders are loners who understand that they don't do well in normal society. Even in Alaska they flee cities like Anchorage and Fairbanks, hoping to outrun their own anger or mental illness, to live without the irritant of other human beings. A lot of these people succeed but many can't run far enough or fast enough. Louis Hastings sought refuge in a defunct mining town, then shot most of his neighbors. Michael Silka managed to murder seven people along a river bank 120 miles from Fairbanks before people noticed that their friends were disappearing.

Yes, husbands and wives kill each other in Alaska, just as they do everywhere. Drug dealers punctuate their commercial disputes with bullets. Gang wannabes shoot rivals from cars, and drunks brawl to the death. Brennan doesn't write about these commonplaces.

Murder fueled by drunken anger or dope is rarely interesting. It doesn't illuminate the frightening ways the human soul can warp. How could fourteen-year-old Winona Fletcher fire a bullet into a seventy-year-old woman begging on her knees for her life? She's never answered the question and it's unlikely we'll ever know for sure. "How could you," and "why would you" are life's real mysteries.

Most of the killers in these stories came to Alaska from somewhere else, perhaps with the same dreams of a better future as the rest of us. But their path led instead to death or a prison cell.

Sheila Toomey
Anchorage

Sheila Toomey has reported on crime in Alaska for 20 years. Her work appears in the Anchorage Daily News, on the Scripps Howard News Service and at www.adn.com.

PREFACE

The research and writing of this book put me in fearful proximity to the dark side of Alaska. Living here, it's easy to accept the popular view of Alaska as a place defined by its magnificent scenery, abundant wildlife, and serenity. But the hard fact is that Alaska is also a place where passion, alienation, or dementia can result in sudden, violent death. The proof lies in these ten stories of murder most foul.

Alaska's climate played a role in some of these cases, as did the state's remote location. Extreme cold, long winter nights—even the continuous sunlight of summer—can affect the minds of those living on the emotional edge. Many of the murderers described here were misfits who retreated from civilization to build new lives in the wilderness, but found the North Country even harder to handle than the societies they left. Eventually the misfits exploded and people died.

These are uniquely Alaskan murder cases, from the novice hunter who goes berserk when the thermometer hits rock bottom, to the pilot and serial killer who flies his victims into the wilderness, rapes and kills them, then buries their bodies in tundra and gravel river bottoms. One killer is a young man who comes to the territory at the turn of the twentieth century to build a railroad, kills a man who attacks his lover, and eventually becomes known to the world as the Birdman of Alcatraz.

The cases range from individual crimes of passion to explosive mass killings and cold-blooded serial butchery. The stories are true and readers may find the details shocking. I was first introduced to Alaska crime in 1967 when I left the Worcester, Massachusetts *Telegram* to become a reporter and columnist for the *Anchorage Times.*

Most of the crimes described here occurred during my many years in Alaska, and I followed each story as it unfolded day by day.

I thought I knew what the killings were all about until I began trying to re-create what happened, putting myself in the shoes of the murderers and their victims. That proved to be a chilling experience beyond all expectation. Immersing oneself in a crime, looking into the minds of those who hate intensely and imagining the fear and horror of the soon-to-die, proved to be unsettling in a way I could not anticipate.

I have tried to provide enough information to enable readers to relive the events themselves. And if I have failed to re-create the real fears and passions of those who were actually there—if I have distanced the reader a little from the experience—you might be grateful.

The ten killers took at least fifty-three lives, perhaps many more. At least thirty-two of the victims were women and twenty-one were men. Some were hit without warning and died quickly; others experienced horror lasting hours. Some had high-risk lifestyles—they were prostitutes or topless dancers living on society's fringe. But others were minding their own business and met their fate while performing innocuous daily chores.

At least five of the female victims were hitchhiking when they met their killers. By using this time-tested means of inexpensive travel, these young women were in effect trolling for psychopaths. They demonstrated their fearlessness and openness to adventure, but the simple gesture of holding out their thumbs led to their deaths. The murderers were all too willing to stop and offer them rides.

The quality of police work involved here ranged from brilliant to blockheaded, and in some cases investigators could do nothing more than arrest the killers, clean up the scene, and try to figure out what happened. But solving some of the crimes required dogged and thoughtful probing, resulting in the capture of murderers who might otherwise have gone free to kill again. Many of the officers put their lives on the line in pursuing killers, and in one case—that of Trooper Troy Duncan—the officer laid down that life.

Each of the sensational murder cases dissected here was ultimately solved, generating enough details to make it possible to put the reader on the scene. Necessarily, many cases were left out of the book, including several of Alaska's most notorious crimes: the killing of Independence Party leader Joe Vogler; the rape and murder of eleven-year-old Mandy Lemaire; the car-bomb murder of Muriel Pfeil and the shooting of her brother Robert; the slaying of eight people aboard the vessel *Investor.* These cases were left out because the frightening details of those murders remain known only to the killers themselves. Many of the re-creations in the ten cases covered in *Murder at Forty Below* were possible because investigators dug until the truth came out. They dug until they could tell the world what really happened.

ACKNOWLEDGMENTS

Doing research for this book was an intensive effort that required help from many people. I would especially like to thank a number of Alaska State Troopers, both those retired and others still active, who were involved in these cases and provided vital background information and assistance. The list includes former Trooper Director and Colonel Tom Anderson, retired Major Walt Gilmour, retired Lieutenant John Meyers, the late Captain Jerry Williams, retired Sergeant James McCann, former Trooper Lorry Schuerch, active Captain Chris Stockard, and Jeanne Shaindlin of the Troopers' community affairs office.

Contributions are also gratefully acknowledged from Bob Lee, innkeeper and postmaster at Manley Hot Springs; *Anchorage Daily News* reporter Sheila Toomey, who wrote the foreword to this book and covered many of the murder cases as they occurred; *Daily News* Editor Pat Dougherty and Librarian Sharon Palmisano, who gave me access to the files of the *Daily News* and the *Anchorage Times;* and *Anchorage Times* editor Paul Jenkins, a man with a long memory. Thanks also to the editor of this book, Don Graydon, and publisher Kent Sturgis, who provided support and encouragement throughout the project.

Much of the information on which this book is based came from newspaper clippings, police and court files, interviews with investigators, Internet sources, and a variety of historical publications. Source books included *Butcher, Baker,* by Walter Gilmour and Leland E. Hale (Onyx, 1991); *Fair Game,* by Bernard DuClos (St. Martin's Paperbacks, 1993);

Birdman of Alcatraz, by Thomas E. Gaddis (1955; Comstock Editions printing, 1989); and the *Alaska State Troopers Golden Anniversary Book,* by Jerry Williams (Alaska State Troopers Anniversary Committee, 1991).

Some of the various accounts, particularly those regarding Robert Stroud, contradicted each other. In Stroud's case the accounts tended to follow one of two tracks: those writers who accepted the Birdman of Alcatraz as a brilliant and badly treated victim of injustice and those who sided with corrections officials in considering him a troublesome prisoner who deserved what he got. In each case I accepted for this book the versions that I judged most credible.

chapter one

THE TROPHY HUNTER

At first, police weren't alarmed when topless dancers began to vanish. Such disappearances could be good news or bad. Some girls were rescued from life on the edge. Others died from drug overdoses.

Robert Hansen seemed a true Alaska outdoorsman and good neighbor. He was a big-game hunter, owned an airplane, and was a family man who enjoyed outings with his friends. He was a churchgoing business owner with a well-stocked trophy room, an intense person who worked and played hard. He was not unknown to police, had actually done time in prison, but his problems appeared to be a combination of youthful indiscretion and adult dustups with prostitutes. He seemed to have overcome his behavior slips and was doing quite well.

When he came to police attention, Hansen's minister and hunting buddies spoke up for him. When charges were brought, he hired one of Alaska's best criminal lawyers. Robert Hansen was a very skillful liar, one so accomplished that he could convince good people that he was a well-intentioned man with a few foibles. He was, Hansen made them believe, a man of good character who sometimes went astray, who perhaps needed psychiatric counseling but certainly not imprisonment. What neither his defenders nor anybody else knew about for a frighteningly long time was his consuming and horrific hobby. He was hunting more than animals.

Anchorage was a thriving place in the 1970s. The pipeline boom was in full swing and money flowed, swelling the city's population and bringing new opportunity. Those thronging north included young men and women looking for new lives, adventure, and a chance to make money. Among them were entrepreneurs of all kinds, everything from oil and real estate speculators to mobsters, some in hard hats, some in business suits.

Racketeers were invisible at first. Fourth Avenue had been the center of the city's seamy side since the boom days of World War II and remained unchanged through the discovery of oil at Swanson River on the Kenai Peninsula in 1957 and the heady days of statehood that followed. Boom times came and fell away, but Alaska always grew, only the pace changing. And always, through good times and bad, bored and lonely people gathered on Fourth Avenue in search of a good time.

The avenue was called the longest bar in the world. It was home to row on row of taverns, close enough to allow continuous barhopping without fighting the weather. In the 1970s, Fourth Avenue drew nude dancers, prostitutes, and the hard-drinking men who were flooding in to build the pipeline and get in on the action.

The topless bars had names like the Wild Cherry, the Booby Trap, the Embers, the Red Garter, and the

Good Times Lounge. Many were owned or controlled by Frank Colacurcio, a Seattle mobster who ran a topless bar and pornography network from his cell at the McNeil Island federal penitentiary in Puget Sound, Washington. His Alaska clubs—and most of the few independents remaining in Anchorage—hired young women through Talents West, a Colacurcio-owned booking agency.

The women of Fourth Avenue lived a high-risk lifestyle. They were nominally hired for their ability to dance, though none were asked to audition. The recruiters selected them solely for their age, their looks, and their interest in coming north. Virtually all were jobless, many had drug or alcohol addictions, some were innocents wanting to try a fling on the wild side. They had one thing in common: all came for the money. Recruiters told them a dancer's pay and tips could easily reach five hundred dollars per day, not counting what they might make on the side for whatever they chose to do.

During work hours the girls danced half-naked, hustled drinks, and entertained customers with table dances. Such dances entailed rhythmic presentations of their intimate assets pressed close to the client's face and shaken to loud music and pulsing strobe lights. The dances often resulted in large tips, a major portion of the dancer's income, and could cause a stratospheric rise in the customer's libido, putting the client in need of a prostitute or a bucket of cold water.

Women commonly disappeared from Fourth Avenue. Some disappearances resulted from overdoses of drugs or alcohol, some from misadventure. A few women grew disgusted with their lives and slipped away to Seattle. Church groups rescued others, spiriting them out of Alaska to safe and distant havens. The disappeared were sometimes reported missing by friends and roommates who had not been told about any plans to leave.

Police were not alarmed when dancers went missing from Fourth Avenue. Vanished girls could be either good news or bad news, depending on where they went and how. Worst case, it could mean that a girl had overdosed on drugs. If not found sooner, her body would turn up when the snow melted. If a dancer died, it was sad but not surprising; after all, they lived high-risk lives. The thing about living on the edge is that sometimes you fell—or were pushed—over that edge.

Robert Hansen was born in Esterville, Iowa, on February 15, 1939. His family later moved to California but returned seven years later and settled in Pocahontas, 125 miles northwest of Des Moines. Bob began work in his father's bakery while still in grammar school. He stuttered, had severe acne, and was left-handed. His parents thought left-handedness to be an aberration and pushed him to use his right hand. Their pressure didn't help his manual dexterity much, but it did make his stutter worse.

Bob's speech problem was humiliating. During his junior high and high school years, his peers—both boys and girls—sometimes laughed and mocked his inability to express himself. He hid his feelings, but later psychiatric studies suggested he was developing feelings of failure and inadequacy and a seething anger.

He started high school in 1953, a time when others his age were socializing at sock hops and dance parties made more raucous and fun with the birth of rock and roll. But his long hours at the bakery, strictly religious parents, and a lack of money kept him out of the action. He became a reluctant loner, an outcast whose isolation fed his internal fury.

He had marginal success in sports, failing to make the basketball and football teams but winning a solitary letter in track during his senior year. He enjoyed hunting, fishing, and archery, all solitary activities he could pursue outdoors, where he preferred to be.

After graduation in 1957, Hansen joined the Army Reserves and underwent basic training at Fort Dix, New Jersey. One weekend he was randomly selected as the USO's Soldier of the Week, which earned him an expense-paid trip to New York City. There he teamed up with another young soldier and sought out a pair of prostitutes. The soldiers found the whores disinterested in the liaisons, and the encounters to be perfunctory and unsatisfying.

Hansen received advanced training as a military police officer at Fort Knox, Kentucky, and frequently visited prostitutes in the nearby community. He later told an interviewer "it was strictly slam, bam, thank you ma'am." He was dissatisfied with quickie sex and yearned to "take control of the situation."

After military training, he returned to Iowa and his father's bakery. In 1959 he dated the daughter of the town's chiropractor. The girl came from a family as reclusive as his own. That same year the town of Pocahontas formed a Junior Police. Thirty young people were sworn in and the chief of police introduced their drill instructor, Robert Hansen. Shortly afterward Bob's father hired the son of a jeweler to help out in the bakery. The boy was a quiet, crew-cut sixteen-year-old, someone Bob felt he could control.

On December 7, 1960, the town's volunteer fire department raced to the bus barn at the local Catholic school. One end of the building was already engulfed in flames, so the firefighters tried to save the buses. As one fireman drove a bus through the flames and into the clear air outside, its gas tank exploded, sending him flying out of the vehicle, covered with cuts and burns. All but three of the buses were saved but the building burned, as did athletic equipment, stored desks, stage props, and tools. Among those manning the hoses that night was volunteer fireman Robert Hansen.

The fire marshal concluded that the blaze was arson. A three-month investigation turned up no leads until the police chief received a call from a sixteen-year-old with a nagging conscience. It was the jeweler's son, Hansen's bakery co-worker. The boy told the chief that Hansen had told him several times that he intended to burn the bus barn just to see if he could get away with it. He wanted to settle a score with the school superintendent, who had disciplined him on several occasions.

The boy said Hansen had talked him into the scheme, that Hansen had climbed to the barn's loft with a five-gallon can of gasoline and spread the fuel around, then set it afire. They both ran back to the bakery. There they quickly painted an oven and tried to look like they had been working at it through the evening.

Hansen was then getting ready to marry the chiropractor's daughter, but found himself indicted, jailed, and held for $2,500 bail. His mother bailed him out on his wedding day, and the marriage went on as scheduled. That fall he was convicted of arson and sentenced to three years at the state reformatory at Anamosa. Soon after, his bride divorced him.

A prison psychiatrist diagnosed Hansen as "an infantile personality" who imagined doing violence to girls who had rejected and ridiculed him. Hansen told the interviewer he wanted to blow up the town water tower and shoot out the police car's lights. He wanted to get even with everyone.

When Hansen's statements were used against him at a parole hearing, he felt the doctor had violated his confidence. He determined never to be made a sucker again and decided that in future confrontations he would tell interviewers that sometimes he couldn't remember what he had done. He was beginning to learn from his mistakes.

In the reformatory, Hansen worked within the system, assisting a staff counselor and typing letters for inmates who couldn't read or write. He took a correspondence course on the Bible and began religious counseling for his fellow inmates. The staff counselor arranged for speech therapy at the nearby University of Iowa, which gradually erased much of his stutter.

In late 1962, a psychiatrist reported that Hansen still had an infantile personality but that his antisocial attitude was greatly diminished. He was paroled on May 1, 1963, a year early. He had won his freedom by hiding his anger and by good works, another lesson learned.

Embarrassed by their son's arson and jailing, Hansen's parents left Pocahontas and bought a small resort on a fishing lake in northern Minnesota. When Hansen was released from Anamosa, he joined them, working at painting boats and cabins and rigging docks. Later he guided fishing parties and fell in love with wilderness.

At the lake he met a girl from Pocahontas who was on vacation from the University of Iowa. Hansen's parents had hired her to clean cabins. At the end of summer he proposed marriage; Darla said yes and they made plans to marry after her graduation. Hansen took a course in cake decoration and a series of bakery jobs in Minnesota, North Dakota, and South Dakota. But his employers were dismayed to find he was a thief with an explosive temper. At one bakery, he took to hiding all kinds of things around the shop—radios, small appliances, and sporting goods. One suspicious employee took his boss out to look into the back of Hansen's car, where he had seen two bicycles with padlocks still on the wheels.

In 1965 Hansen was arrested for shoplifting from a sporting goods store. When his wife found out, she persuaded the pastor at the Lutheran church to vouch for him. The charges were dropped. A few months later, his boss caught him rifling the bakery's cash drawer. Hansen had come to the shop early and used a knife to break open the office door. When the baker threatened to press charges, Hansen said he had been offered another job and was leaving. The baker sputtered angrily but dropped the matter.

Their outdoor experiences in northern Minnesota grew into a love of the wilderness for both Hansen and his wife. After her university graduation in 1967, they loaded their belongings and a tent into a new Pontiac and headed north to Anchorage. Hansen hired on as a baker and cake decorator at a Safeway store. His wife became a teacher at Government Hill School.

Darla Hansen was active in the Lutheran Church and together they went hiking, camping, climbing, and fishing. Hansen was an avid archer and bow hunter, joining both the Black Sheep Bowmen and the Alaska Archery Association. He began to collect wild game trophies, taking record-class mountain goats, caribou, and Dall sheep. He became friend and hunting buddy to Anchorage insurance man John Sumrall.

When Darla gave birth to a daughter, she stopped participating in his wilderness outings. The couple went to church and social functions together, but they developed separate lives.

In 1971 Hansen killed a big Dall sheep and claimed it as the largest ever taken with a bow. The world record claim was challenged when a tipster charged that the animal was taken in an area closed to hunting and that a firearm was used in the kill. Hansen signed a Fair Chase Affidavit provided by Pope and Young, arbiters of the trophy-hunting world. He swore that no firearm was used; John Sumrall vouched for him.

On November 15, 1971, eighteen-year-old Susie Heppeard was headed home after a morning of shopping. She stopped at a red light on Northern Lights Boulevard in Anchorage and turned to see a man in the next car. She smiled reflexively and then drove to her apartment. There she unloaded her shopping bags and was about to jump into the shower when she heard a knock at her door. She wrapped a towel around herself and went to answer. At the door was the man she had seen in the car at the stoplight. He wore a fluorescent orange cap, a hunter's cap.

The man asked to borrow a phone book, saying he was looking for someone in the apartment complex. Susie pointed to a book on a table by the door. The man riffled through the pages, then said his friend must be unlisted. He tried to strike up a conversation, but Susie backed away. He asked her for a date and she told him, "I'm engaged." The man left.

A week later, Susie swung into her driveway in early morning and saw a man wearing an orange cap duck behind a nearby building. When she got out of the car, the man stepped out, pointed a gun in her face, and muttered: "Shut up, sweetheart, or I'll blow your brains out."

She screamed. The man cocked the pistol and said, "Scream again and I'll blow your head off."

Susan Scott looked out a nearby window. She saw a man standing with her roommate at the base of the stairs, holding what looked like a gun. Scott opened the door and called down, "What's going on, Susie? Are you all right?" Their other roommate, Frances Lake, awakened and came to the living room, where Scott was then calling the police.

"What's going on?" Lake asked. "I thought I heard a scream."

"You did. I think that guy may be going to rape Susie."

Lake opened the door and shouted, "Susie, get away from that jerk! We've called the police."

The man shoved the gun into Susie Heppeard's back and forced her toward the street. Hearing the wail of an approaching siren, he disappeared into the darkness.

Susie was terrified. When police officers leaped from their patrol car with guns drawn, she fell to the ground, shrieking: "He said he was going to blow my head off!"

While Susie was giving the man's description to one officer, Alaska's first canine police unit began tracking her would-be rapist through the snow. Officer Archie Hutchins and his dog found Robert Hansen walking through the icy darkness in shirtsleeves. Hansen told the officer he had been driving, felt woozy, and pulled over to get some fresh air. A patrolman found a loaded .22-caliber pistol under the driver's seat of Hansen's car. Hutchins and the dog followed Hansen's trail backward and found an orange hat in the snow and a .357 Magnum revolver on top of a tire in the wheel well of an abandoned car. Hansen admitted that the hat and the .357 were similar to ones he owned. The tips of the bullets in the .357 had been creased with a knife, creating what are called dum-dum shells, bullets that expand rapidly and smash into their targets with devastating impact.

When Susie saw Hansen in the rear of the patrol car, she said: "That's him."

Hansen told police that he might have been involved in the incident with Susie Heppeard, but had no memory of it. "If I was," he said, "I need help."

Hansen was charged with assault with a deadly weapon. Defense attorney James Gilmore requested that

Hansen be examined at the Langdon Psychiatric Clinic and released on his own recognizance. The prosecutor objected, noting that Hansen had threatened Susie Heppeard's life. He asked that bail be set at $2,000.

At that point, opinions about Hansen within the police community and the court system began to diverge widely. Jim Gilmore was one of Alaska's best defense lawyers and argued in court that Hansen had been married eight years, had a child, and owned property; he was a man of substance with roots in the community. At the same time, Hansen's bizarre behavior and dum-dum bullets brought him a place of honor in what police called "the asshole book," a list of local characters whom officers kept track of and checked on when bad things happened. The keeper of the asshole book was Anchorage homicide investigator Ron Rice, who was learning the art of criminal profiling. Bad Bob the Baker, as investigators came to call Hansen, was gaining a reputation.

Hansen was released on his own recognizance with the stipulation that he could have no contact with Susie Heppeard. In mid-December, a grand jury charged him with assault with a deadly weapon. Just three days later, Hansen kidnapped an eighteen-year-old topless dancer who had stopped for a 4:00 a.m. cup of tea at the Nevada Cafe on Gambell Street. Hansen tried unsuccessfully to pick her up, then pulled a pistol and ordered her into his Pontiac. While driving through South Anchorage, Hansen spotted a police car. "There goes your help," he told her. "Look," he said, "if we get stopped by the cops, don't do or say anything, or I'll have to shoot them. Understand?"

She nodded in terror.

Hansen then tied her hands and ankles with shoe-laces, shoving her forcefully onto the car's floor. He drove down the Seward Highway past McHugh Creek to Indian and parked on a secluded dead-end road. Hansen noticed black lace on her bra, which showed from her ruined blouse. To her surprise, he asked calmly if he could rip off the bra. She asked him not to, saying it had been expensive. Instead he untied her hands and ordered her to take off both her dress and bra. "You won't run if you're naked," he said.

The young woman then persuaded Hansen to drive to Portage for cigarettes, after which he drove to the Kenai Peninsula and rented a cabin at the Sunrise Inn; there he raped her. During the drive back to Anchorage, he abruptly turned the car around and headed south once again. Hansen told her he wanted to look at a cabin where he had taken a girl the weekend before. A heavy snow blocked Cooper Lake Road, forcing him to turn back. Midway down the mountainous road, he stopped the car, ordered her out, cocked his pistol, and said: "Start running."

The woman pleaded with Hansen, telling him he was handsome and good in bed and that they could date. She told him about her baby son, who would lose his mother if she died. Hansen said he couldn't let her go because she could turn him in to the police. He relented but found her parents' names and address in her purse and wrote them down. Their names were his insurance for her silence. He told her that if she talked, he would kill her parents and her son.

Eventually he dropped her back in Anchorage a few blocks from her car. She found it and climbed in, shaking. Had Hansen dug further into her purse, he would have found her father's business card and probably killed her. Her dad was an Alaska State Trooper.

The young dancer was determined not to involve police; she was afraid Hansen might fulfill his threats.

She changed her mind on Christmas Day when two young men found the half-naked body of a college freshman in a ravine at McHugh Creek Campground, a few miles from the spot Hansen had taken her. The woman's hands had been tied behind her back with wire; she had been raped and her chest had been slashed. Investigators concluded she had been alive when she was thrown or fell into the ravine, perhaps while escaping her attacker. The woman had been unable to climb the steep slope and froze to death.

The dancer fearfully concluded that the McHugh Creek murder might have been Hansen's work. She went to state trooper headquarters, identified him from file photos, and told her story. Hansen was arrested again and new charges were added to those already filed against him. When he was booked at the Alaska State Jail, a rookie correctional officer was behind the desk. The arresting officers handed the rookie a plastic bag containing Hansen's wallet and the contents of his pockets. The desk officer counted out the money from the wallet, made a note of it, then put the money back. Hansen asked to get into his wallet for a minute, saying he thought there might be hidden money that needed to be logged. The officer handed him the wallet, then was distracted briefly, but turned back in time to see Hansen hiding a crushed piece of paper in a corner of his hand.

When the booking officer's co-worker returned to fingerprint the suspect, the rookie told him about the palmed paper and suggested that the prisoner be searched again. The paper was found wadded in one of his pockets. Hansen said it was the name of someone who would bail him out, so the officer hand-copied the name and address that were on the paper, then handed it back. By the time the officers realized that the name and address were those Hansen had copied from the dancer's pocketbook—the parents he had threatened to kill—Hansen had already eaten the original paper and the officer couldn't prove he had copied it from the scrap found on the prisoner.

On December 29, Hansen was arraigned and ordered held on $50,000 bail. At a preliminary hearing January 7, Hansen's lawyer attacked the young dancer's credibility and provided three character witnesses: Hansen's family minister, the Rev. Albert L. Abrahamson, pastor of Lutheran Central Church; and two hunting buddies, John Sumrall and Gerald Goldschmidt, an environmental health officer for the Alaska Native Health Service.

The dancer proved to be a nervous and uncertain witness. Jim Gilmore's questioning tore holes in her testimony; her veracity was weakened by her topless dancing career and experimentation with drugs. All three of the character witnesses said Bob Hansen would not harm anyone. Goldschmidt thought the dancer must have been mistaken. The witnesses urged that their friend and parishioner be returned to his family.

The young dancer was never publicly identified. A few months after the trial, the charges in her case were dropped in plea-bargaining and Hansen received a five-year sentence for assaulting Susie Heppeard. He would become eligible for parole when deemed psychologically fit. A psychiatrist testified that Hansen was schizophrenic and could commit violent acts without being able to remember them. He said Hansen's condition was treatable and recommended twice-a-week psychiatric counseling and close supervision.

Hansen was a model prisoner and, in less than three months, won transfer to a halfway house. He was given psychiatric treatment and placed on work release. Years later he told investigators that while on work release he would often drive to downtown Anchorage, park, and watch prostitutes walking the streets. "I'd get a tremendous gosh dang," he bragged, saying the activity gave him a "sexual blowup charge." He said that even in jail he had been thinking about being free to pursue women again.

At the end of November, he was freed from the halfway house and returned home to his family, where his wife had found solace in her religion. Hansen's imprisonment, his keen mind, and his devious nature had taught him how to tell jailers and psychiatrists what they wanted to hear, what they were looking for as signs of improvement. And his skills as a convincing liar were finely honed. He also secretly decided that letting his victims live had been a big mistake, a mistake he would not make again. Dead women could not testify against him and send him back to prison. "We taught the guy to kill," recalled Trooper Major Walt Gilmour in an interview years later. "Now he is back on the streets and knows he needs to kill."

The early 1970s were a tumultuous time in Anchorage. The Vietnam War was winding down and Alaska was gearing up to build the trans-Alaska oil pipeline. Both the major oil companies drilling in the Arctic oilfields and the consortium assembled to the build the pipeline were headquartered in Anchorage. The city's population grew rapidly with oil executives and contractors flooding in to take jobs and bid for work. Behind them were war veterans and construction workers anxious to find high-paying jobs. And behind them all came whores, pimps, and criminals hoping to take their money.

Anchorage was experiencing growing pains reminiscent of the Gold Rush and the World War II economic boom. For the first time, the city found itself dealing with city limits that arbitrarily ended in what was becoming known as Mid-town. The rest of the Anchorage Bowl, including the residential Hillside, the business district of South Anchorage, and suburbs to the north and south were all part of the Greater Anchorage Area Borough. The Anchorage Police Department provided protection in the city itself. Alaska State Troopers, with a smaller force, had responsibility for virtually the entire state of Alaska, including the area inside the Anchorage Borough but outside the city.

Criminals learned that their activities were much more likely to be discovered and themselves arrested if they operated in the more intensely policed city limits. Even those who had dance clubs on Fourth Avenue found they had far more freedom with satellite clubs in the area patrolled by the hard-pressed State Troopers. "We had rows and rows and rows of Cadillacs," Walt Gilmour said in an interview, "driven by bad people who came to town and moved outside the city into the trooper area."

Hansen owned a thirty-six-foot cabin cruiser, which he moored in the small boat harbor at Seward, 125 miles south of Anchorage. He used it for hunting and fishing trips, sometimes with his buddies, occasionally taking along his wife, Darla.

On July 7, 1973, seventeen-year-old Megan Emerick was doing her washing in the self-service laundry of a dormitory at the Seward Skill Center. She folded and put away her clothes, ran a brush through her long, blond hair, and left the dorm. She was never seen again. Police believe her body lies in a shallow grave on the shore of Seward's Resurrection Bay, somewhere near one of two spots on the bay that were marked by an X on an aviation map that was later found stuffed behind the headboard of Hansen's bed.

In early summer of 1975, twenty-three-year-old Mary K. Thill accepted a ride with friends from her home at Lowell Point into Seward. They dropped her off, and she disappeared forever. Her body is also believed buried on Resurrection Bay near one of the Xs on Hansen's map.

A few weeks later, Hansen went carousing at the Kit Kat Club on Old Seward Highway. He flashed a roll of bills and said he'd just arrived in the state to help build the trans-Alaska pipeline. A dancer agreed to meet him; when she climbed into his car, he roughed her up, put a pistol to her head, and drove to the edge of Chugach State Park. There he raped her, then let her go.

The woman reported the rape but refused to file charges. She was a schoolteacher from another state who had come to Alaska to make money, didn't want the embarrassment, and quickly left town. A State Trooper investigated and learned the auto license number she had given belonged to Hansen. The trooper notified Hansen's parole officer, but Hansen claimed he thought he and the dancer were on a date. "Then she asked for money, and I refused to pay," he said. "So she gets mad and hollers rape." It was a story Hansen would use many times. The parole officer didn't believe him, but the woman was gone and he could prove nothing.

In November 1976, a security guard at the Fred Meyer Store in Anchorage caught Hansen trying to shoplift a chain saw. Because of his prior record, he was charged with larceny in a building, a more serious offense than shoplifting. He told the judge he didn't have enough money to buy the chain saw but wanted to send it to his elderly father, who was ailing. Hansen said he had first left the store without the saw but then witnessed a man being treated for a heart attack in the parking lot. Hansen said he thought of his father's bad heart and approaching birthday, then returned to the store and stole the saw. "I know what I did was wrong," he said, "and I'm very sorry for doing so."

Judge James K. Singleton sentenced him to five years in prison. Hansen was sent to the Juneau Correctional Institute and released sixteen months later, after the Alaska Supreme Court reviewed his case. The court's legal opinion noted that Hansen's previous offenses were five and fifteen years before the chain saw theft and that he "has maintained steady employment, been a good provider, and has earned the reputation of a hard worker and a respectable member of the community."

In each of his jailings, psychiatric reports suggested that Hansen was disturbed and potentially dangerous, but his antisocial behavior seemed to respond to drugs like lithium. When Judge Singleton ordered his release, he noted angrily: "I'm absolutely convinced that Mr. Hansen is going to commit additional crimes. But in this case the Supreme Court has indicated that as long as the crimes are against property, not crimes of violence, the community is just going to have to tolerate it." The judge's statement was puzzling since Hansen had gone to prison five years earlier for his assault on Susie Heppeard.

Singleton ordered that Hansen receive psychiatric and drug treatment, but the assistant district attorney responsible for the case never followed through with the order. Hansen received no further treatment and his parole was unsupervised. Just a few weeks after his release, he murdered a woman at Summit Lake on the Kenai Peninsula.

The Summit Lake killing, which Hansen later admitted to investigators, resulted from an important change in his method. Hansen's latest arrest and jailing had been painful and he was determined to avoid any repeat. The shoplifting bust was one thing, but many of his legal problems related to women. He had been caught in the past because of dancers who lived to testify against him. He knew a way to fix that problem: kill them all. A series of abductions, rapes, and murders followed. Most were reported as club dancers and prostitutes gone missing. Their disappearances were investigated, but police couldn't be sure they didn't just skip out without telling anyone. The women left belongings behind, but those never amounted to much.

Meanwhile Hansen opened a bakery of his own near downtown Anchorage. The business thrived and in July 1982 he used bakery cash and an insurance settlement to buy a small airplane, a SuperCub, ideal for wilderness flying. He did not have a pilot's license; he was refused one because he was taking lithium. But Hansen learned to fly illicitly. He became a skilled if illegal pilot and found the airplane added a thrilling new dimension to his deadly hobby of hunting women.

At first his hunts took place primarily in spring and summer, but by the time the years-long spree finally ended, he was stalking women every few weeks. His list of murders included:

• An unidentified prostitute believed to have come to Anchorage from Kodiak, and dubbed Eklutna Annie by police. Sometime in the fall of 1979, Hansen cut a deal with her for sex and she climbed into his camper. He told her they were going to his home, but he drove instead to Eklutna Road, a remote area where he often hunted bears. When she realized he was heading out of town, she became nervous and demanded he go back. He pulled a gun and continued driving.

When his truck became stuck in a mudhole, Hansen rigged a winch, then ordered her to work the cable while he drove. After many tries, the truck popped free. When Hansen climbed back behind the wheel, she ran for the woods. He leaped out, chased her down, and grabbed her by the hair. She pulled a large hunting knife and swung at him, but he grabbed her arm and tripped her to the ground. She was lying face down, screaming hysterically, when he plunged the knife into her back. He buried her in a shallow grave below a power line. The body was found the following July 8 but could not be identified, and no clues were found to her murder.

• Joanne Messina, a cannery worker whom Hansen met on the dock in Seward. He bought her dinner at the Harbor View Restaurant. Later, in his camper, she propositioned him. He drove up the Seward Highway to the Snow River. She grew anxious and demanded he head back to Seward. They fought and she leaped from the camper. He grabbed a .22 pistol, caught up with her, and whacked her on the head. When she fought back, he killed her with two shots, dragged her body to a gravel pit, and covered it with sand and rock.

Messina had brought her dog with her. Hansen shot the dog and threw it into the woods, then dumped Messina's camping gear behind it and tossed the pistol into the Snow River. Seward police found her decomposing remains the following month; bears had eaten half her torso.

• Roxanne Easlund, newly arrived from Seattle and living at the Budget Motel in Anchorage. On June 28, 1980, she went to meet a date on Northern Lights Boulevard and never returned. Four days later her roommate filed a missing persons report.

• Lisa Futrell, a dancer from Hawaii working at the Great Alaskan Bush Company. Her last dance was September 6, 1980, a night when Robert Hansen watched her while sipping a beer. Troopers found her body in a gravel pit near the old Knik River bridge just north of Anchorage, covered by six inches of leaves and soil.

• Sherry Morrow, a dancer at the Wild Cherry. Morrow left a friend's house on November 17, 1981, saying she was going to Alice's 210 Cafe to meet a photographer who was going to pay her three hundred dollars for posing nude.

When Morrow climbed into his Subaru, he handcuffed her, blindfolded her with an Ace bandage, and forced her to kneel on the floor of the car. He drove north to the Knik River and tried to remove the handcuffs, but she began kicking and screaming. He took a short-barreled semi-automatic rifle out of the car's trunk and sat by a tree, waiting for her to cool off. But the angry woman ran to him and resumed kicking and screaming. "I just pointed the Mini-14 up toward her and pulled the trigger," he said.

He dug a shallow grave in the riverbed and took Morrow's arrowhead necklace as a souvenir. He picked up the spent .223 shell casing, tossed it into the grave, and covered her with dirt.

• Andrea Altiery, who was killed two weeks after the Morrow murder. Altiery had hugged her roommate and left their apartment, saying she was meeting an older man who had offered to take her on a shopping spree at the Boniface Mall. Hansen ultimately told her story as well. He drove her, handcuffed and blindfolded, to a spot near the Knik River railroad bridge. He told Altiery that he had raped a woman there the week before; that the woman had been cooperative and he had let her go afterward.

In the car he fondled Altiery's breasts while holding a pistol to her head and forcing her to give him oral sex. When Altiery said she had to go to the bathroom, they got out of the car and he laid the gun on the car's hood. Hansen turned to urinate while she walked a distance away. He heard a noise and turned back to see her reaching for the pistol. He grabbed it. When she started clawing at his face and poking her fingers behind his glasses, he shot her.

Hansen took a pearl ring and fish charm necklace as souvenirs, then filled a canvas duffel bag with gravel and dragged it onto the railroad trestle. He tied the bag to Altiery's neck and pushed her body off the trestle into the river.

• Sue Luna, a dancer at the Good Times bar. On May 26, 1982, Luna told her roommate she was meeting a man at Alice's 210 Cafe, a man who had offered her three hundred dollars for an hour of fooling around. The roommate and Luna's sister reported her missing four days later. What was left of her was found two years later where Hansen had buried her, near a parking lot at the Knik River bridge.

• Tami Pederson, also a dancer. In early August 1982, Pederson packed her dance costumes into a suitcase and left to meet a photographer who had promised her three hundred dollars for a photo session. Her remains were found two years later under river gravel near the grave of Sherry Morrow.

• Angela Feddern vanished from Fourth Avenue in February 1983, leaving a five-year-old daughter in Fairbanks and a mother in Seattle. She wasn't reported missing until May. Investigators found her remains a year later at Figure Eight Lake in the Susitna Basin, across Cook Inlet from Anchorage.

• Tereasa Watson, a young prostitute who left to meet a john on March 25, 1983. Hansen flew her to Scenic Lake on the Kenai Peninsula, landing on the ice. He couldn't dig a grave in the frozen ground, so instead left her body where it fell. When found the following year, the corpse had been half-eaten by animals.

• DeLynn Frey, a twenty-year-old blonde whom Hansen flew to a gravel bar on the Knik River in April 1983. She wasn't reported missing until early September. A pilot practicing landings on the gravel found what was left of her sixteen months after she disappeared.

• Paula Goulding, a dancer at the Great Alaska Bush Company who disappeared April 25, 1983. Her body was found the following September in a shallow grave on the Knik River.

As the pace of disappearances accelerated in 1982 and 1983, the Anchorage rumor mill churned wildly and police speculated whether the incidents might be connected—and whether a serial murderer might be stalking the city's topless clubs. The bodies of Joanne Messina and Eklutna Annie had been discovered, but the locations were widely separated and there appeared to be no connection between the two. Then on September 13, 1982, two Anchorage police officers on an off-duty moose hunt found the remains of Sherry Morrow protruding from a Knik River sandbar. They reported the find to State Troopers, who had jurisdiction because of the location outside the Anchorage city limits. In the grave with Morrow's remains were the Ace bandage blindfold and a spent .223 bullet casing.

State Trooper Sergeant Lyle Haugsven, one of the investigators who responded to the call from the two moose hunters, was curious about the many instances of missing dancers. He compiled records on the women and developed a suspect list. Because women had reported strange encounters with Hansen, the baker made the list, but he was one of more than thirty names at that point. Some of the reports came from representatives of the group Standing Together Against Rape, who told Haugsven about a man who was abusive to call girls and refused to pay for services received. STAR declined to identify the complainants, saying the call girls had made their reports on condition of secrecy. The descriptions passed on by STAR sounded a lot like Robert Hansen.

As winter turned to spring, Anchorage city police concluded from a lack of new leads that the murder of Sherry Morrow was an isolated crime and that her murderer had probably left the state. They decided that continuing the investigation under those circumstances would be pointless.

Then, on June 13, a truck driver slammed on his brakes when a handcuffed and barefoot woman ran into the street from a parking lot near Merrill Field in Anchorage. Behind her ran a man with a gun. She climbed into the truck and the driver pulled away. At her insistence, he dropped her at a nearby motel. He then sped to police headquarters. Anchorage officer Gregg Baker found the woman in a room at the Big Timber Motel, still wearing the handcuffs and very much in shock.

The woman told Baker a man kidnapped her and took her to his home. There he raped her and chained her in a room filled with hunting trophies. Later he drove her to Merrill Field and tried to force her into his airplane, telling her they were flying to a remote cabin. Officer Baker drove her to the airfield, where she pointed to a parked airplane. It was Bad Bob Hansen's SuperCub.

Two police officers met Hansen when he drove up to his home. They brought him to headquarters, then searched his home and airplane. They found a variety of hunting guns, but no real evidence. Hansen said he had been visiting at the home of insurance man John Sumrall during the time the woman claimed she was being raped, then spent the balance of the night at the home of another friend, John Henning. Sumrall and Henning confirmed his story. They said Hansen was a respectable businessman who owned a bakery, a home, several cars, and an airplane. He had a wife and two children, who were then en route to Europe.

Investigators wondered if the woman had invented her story, which was strange by any standard. She refused to take a polygraph test. The prosecutor's office dropped the case for lack of evidence that a crime had been committed, and the investigation was shut down. Before Anchorage police closed out the case, one of the officers forwarded the information he had collected to State Troopers. It wound up on the desk of Sergeant Lyle Haugsven, who was still investigating the discovery of Sherry Morrow's body on the Knik River.

On September 2, another body was found on the Knik River, this one quite close to Sherry Morrow's rude grave. In the hole with the new body was another .223 shell casing. Haugsven was away on leave, so Trooper Sergeant Glenn Flothe was assigned to work full time on the Knik River murders. Flothe was a crack investigator who had sat in on Haugsven's weekly briefings on the case. He was an unusual officer, a trained policeman with the mind of an engineer. He was, in the words of his friend and supervisor Walt Gilmour, "what you want a police officer to be." Flothe had studied engineering at the University of Alaska Anchorage before joining the State Troopers and brought his methodical engineer's approach to his work there. Lacking any hot leads in the dancer murders, Flothe laid out all the available evidence on a grid, lining it out in a logical sequence to see where it led.

Finding the second body was convincing evidence that a serial murderer was at work. And the incident at Merrill Field moved Hansen's name well up on the list of possible suspects. Flothe's grid pointed to Hansen, so he ran the man's name through the computer that the agency had acquired as a modern, more effective, and more politically correct information repository than the old "asshole book." The computer showed no record for Hansen, but then Flothe asked Walt Gilmour if he knew anything of the man.

Gilmour remembered Hansen's name coming up in cases involving dancers from the early 1970s. "Is he a pimply faced guy with a stutter?" he asked. When Flothe said the description fit, Gilmour said the computer was wrong.

Because of a flaw in the computer program, Hansen's name had been automatically dropped out of the system due to a lack of recent complaints. Though the officers didn't know it at the time, there had been no recent complaints because Hansen's victims weren't living to tell their tales. Gilmour urged Flothe to dig out the earlier paper files on the Susie Heppeard case, among others. Suddenly Hansen moved to the top of the suspect list.

The investigation and police suspicions became public when Associated Press writer Paul Jenkins heard about an unusual weekend search on the Knik River. Haugsven told Jenkins that troopers were trying to assemble a psychological profile of the killer. Jenkins did his own investigating and on September 20 his article was published with the headline "Authorities Fear List of Dead Women May Grow." He listed seven women as possible victims; the names were from a list compiled by Flothe.

A twenty-four-hour surveillance was placed on Hansen. Meanwhile Flothe's list of presumed victims reached a total of twenty-two. Flothe sought assistance from the FBI's Behavioral Sciences Division in Quantico, Virginia, the nation's leading laboratory with expertise on serial killers. The FBI sent two agents from Quantico, James Horn and John Douglas. According to the book *Butcher, Baker,* by Walter Gilmour and Leland E. Hale (Penguin Books USA, 1991), the agents reviewed the evidence and told Flothe: "The man you want probably

stutters. Is likely an excellent hunter. His wife is probably religious, and not totally aware of her husband's
activities. He's known as a good provider and
hardworking businessman. He's successful, or at least
we wouldn't be surprised if he is.

"He probably stashes things. Like maybe rings or
jewelry or driver's licenses or maybe clothing. He likes
to keep it close to him, so he can view it in private. He
takes it out and relives the killings. It's a movie in his brain
and the objects he's taken from the scene turn him on. If
he's really into it, the killings are all he thinks about twenty-
four hours a day. Everything else is just a motion to him.
His work, his normal routine, is just a motion. Everything
is wrapped up with murder. His whole life, his whole thinking. He probably plans the kills far in advance."

Flothe found the district attorney's office reluctant
to write a new search warrant for Hansen's house because the troopers had produced no new evidence. Flothe
needed the warrant to look for items on the FBI souvenir
list. He called an old friend and float-trip companion in
the Fairbanks district attorney's office, Pat Doogan, who
flew to Anchorage at his own expense and drafted the
warrant. Together they presented it to Judge Victor
Carlson, who issued the search order based on the legal
theory that it was justified to seek evidence of a continuing criminal enterprise.

Troopers searched Hansen's bakery and his home
while Flothe and other officers interviewed the baker at
trooper headquarters. Behind the headboard of his bed
they found an aviation map covered with twenty-four X
marks, some of them at locations where bodies had been
found. When confronted with the map, Hansen said the
marks represented places where he had made touch-

and-go practice landings in his airplane. By itself, the map meant nothing. If he could land there, so could any skilled flier. Throughout the interview, Hansen asked the same question in several ways: "Why is everybody picking on me?"

Flothe had stuck his neck way out on the case, and so had people like Pat Doogan, Judge Carlson, Flothe's supervisors, and his fellow officers. "It's like being the point man in a jungle patrol," Gilmour said. "If things go wrong, you're the first one to get shot—and everybody else is mad at you." Flothe by then was totally convinced that Hansen was the murderer, but he still couldn't prove it. He needed one more vital piece of evidence, if it existed: the stash of mementos. Finding it would put the final nail in the case against Hansen.

Flothe's enthusiasm motivated many other officers to pitch in and try to break the case. One of those was Lieutenant Pat Kasnick, who volunteered to search the attic of Hansen's log home. In the hot and cramped gap beneath the roof, the spaces between the ceiling joists were filled seven inches deep with blown-in pink fiberglass insulation. Carrying a flashlight, his eyes watering furiously and his body sweating, Kasnick crawled through the attic for hours, his hands probing every corner. After combing hundreds of square feet of attic, Kasnick reached once more under the insulation. There, at last, his probing fingers closed on a hollowed-out cache containing several weapons, one of them the .223 rifle used in the murders, and a bag of jewelry taken from the murdered women.

When confronted with the evidence and information about the investigation, Hansen's two alibi witnesses for the Merrill Field incident, John Sumrall and John Henning, admitted they had been lying to protect their buddy. After Hansen was subjected to a series of interrogations over a period of days, his lawyer called and said he "wants to clear the decks." Hansen then confessed.

Hansen admitted to seventeen killings during his twelve-year spree of murder and rape, but investigators believe there were more, perhaps many more. All of the killings to which he confessed involved topless dancers and prostitutes, women he felt were beneath him and deserving of contempt. Some others who disappeared or were murdered during his long rampage were more upright citizens, but Hansen denied involvement in those cases. The list of others included the young coed found tied, half-naked and frozen, at McHugh Creek Campground in 1971. Hansen's aviation map contained no mark at McHugh Creek. The mark might have been missing because the coed had not represented a clean kill. A trophy hunter like Hansen would not boast about a quarry that had escaped and died in the cold.

Hansen did not contest the charges and was not tried. His sentencing hearing lasted just two and a half hours. He chose not to speak or to allow his lawyer to speak for him. Assistant District Attorney Frank Rothschild told the judge:

"Before you sits a monster, an extreme aberration of a human being, a man who walked among us for seventeen years serving us doughnuts, Danish, and coffee with a pleasant smile. His family was a prop; he hid behind decency.

"This hunter who kept trophies on the wall, now has trophies scattered throughout Southcentral Alaska. And while he doesn't talk about or admit to it, it's obvious from looking at where things started and where women ended up, he hunted them down. He'd let them run a little bit, then he enjoyed a hunt, just like with his big-game animals. He toyed with them, he got a charge out of it."

Since Alaska law does not provide for the death penalty, Judge Ralph Moody sentenced Hansen to 461 years plus life, without parole. The judge noted: "There are no words which can adequately describe what we have seen here today, and what the defendant has admitted to. I can't think of a bigger indictment of society than what we have here. This gentleman has been known to us for several years. Yet, we've turned him loose several times knowing that he had the potential to kill."

Hansen is serving his endless sentence at the Spring Creek Correctional Center in Seward.

Robert Hansen has been considered a suspect in some of the Seattle area cases known as the Green River Murders. Two of the troopers interviewed for this book, Colonel Tom Anderson and Major Walt Gilmour, both retired, asked that their suspicions be reported in the hope that a reader might come forward with information about any travels by Hansen to Seattle during the early 1980s.

Two boys riding bicycles over a bridge near Kent, Washington, spotted the first of the Green River victims on July 15, 1982. Within a month, four more bodies were found in or beside the river. All had been strangled and all were killed at different times and left at the murderer's favorite dumping spot. All were prostitutes who plied their trade in a seedy retail district near Seattle-Tacoma International Airport known as the Strip.

The list of dead and missing women eventually climbed to forty-nine. Some of the crimes were committed after Hansen was arrested in late 1983, but the killings involved various methods of operation and body disposal sites. That suggests there may have been more than one murderer. Alaska State Troopers brought their suspicions to detectives in the Green River Task Force, but the Seattle investigators had their own suspects at the time and discounted the Alaskans' suggestion.

Gilmour said the task force couldn't be made to understand the relationship that Alaskans have with Sea-Tac
Airport. Though Anchorage is some 1,400 miles from
Seattle, many Alaskans consider Seattle the city next door,
a place to go even for an occasional long weekend.

None of those considered prime suspects by the
Green River Task Force proved to be the murderer, but
airline passenger manifests and other travel records were
destroyed long ago, leaving no way to track Hansen's travels of the time. Adding to the mystery is the fact that the
driver's license of Marie Malvar, one of the missing, was
found on May 22, 1983, by a janitor cleaning Sea-Tac's
departure gate B4—a gate used at that time by Wien Air
Alaska for flights between Anchorage and Seattle. The
license was turned in to airport police, who notified the
task force. But no attempt was made to claim the license—and check it for fingerprints—for two years. By
that time it had been destroyed.

Any reader with information about Hansen's travels in 1982-83 should contact Alaska State Troopers.

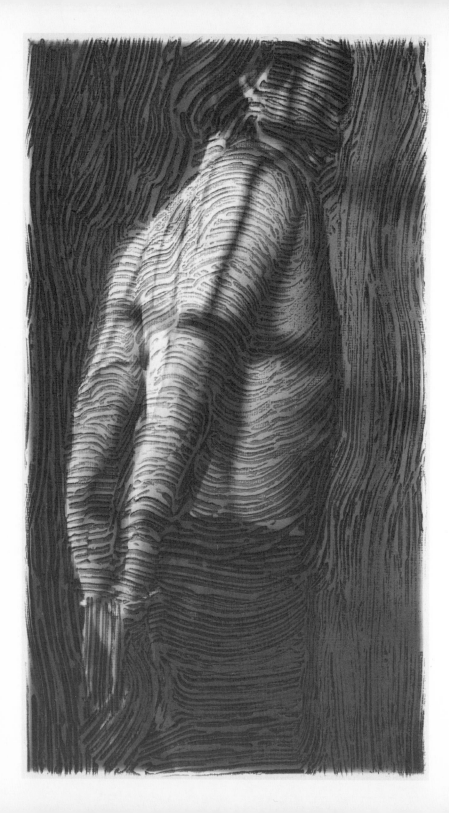

chapter two

BY REASON OF INSANITY

Crazed killer Charles Meach III had resumed drinking and had purchased two pistols, which he hid near the grounds of the Alaska Psychiatric Institute when it was time to check back into the hospital.

Charles L. Meach III was born to a Traverse City, Michigan, dentist and his schizophrenic wife, who spent most of her adult life in a mental hospital. He left Michigan for California at age sixteen, then returned to his father and stepmother's middle-class Midwestern home three years later. Young Meach did not conform well to society's rules. Through the years he developed a record of drug dealing, petty larceny, trespassing, and drunken driving. In 1967 he visited Germany and was arrested there for theft. In the early 1970s he assaulted several people in Michigan, including a former girlfriend, but no charges were filed. At one point his father felt Meach was so much out of control that he needed treatment. The father arranged to have Charles committed to a Michigan mental hospital for three days. After his release, he wandered through several western states, finally making his way to Alaska.

In 1973 Robert Johnson, a twenty-two-year-old grocery bagger, was found beaten to death in Anchorage's Earthquake Park. The young man, a small, mentally retarded person, apparently drowned in his own blood. At first police weren't sure whether he had been beaten to death or run over by a car. Investigators soon learned that several people had seen what they considered a suspicious-looking truck in the area that day, a truck that was soon traced to Charles Meach, who was then twenty-five years old and going through a tough period.

Anchorage Police detective Ralph Christianson was stuck on a weekend shift and found himself questioning the hulking Meach while sitting across a table from him at police headquarters. Meach confessed to kicking the man to death, saying he was drunk and didn't know the victim but was irritated by his voice, which reminded him of Richard Nixon. Meach said he had been unraveling under stress: he had contracted a venereal disease and been rejected by the Army; his truck had been vandalized; he was flunking out of Anchorage Community College.

Meach was jailed and determined by psychiatrists to have paranoid schizophrenia, a mental disorder noted for delusions, hallucinations, an absence of emotion, and distorted thinking. When the case came to court he was charged with first-degree murder but found not guilty by reason of insanity. That meant he would be treated and could be released back to the public when doctors determined he was no longer insane. Since Alaska did not have a secure mental hospital for dangerously violent patients, Meach was sent to the Atascadero facility for the criminally insane in California.

Meach's treatment appeared to be successful. His mental disease went into remission. With an IQ of 125, he was more than smart enough to be able to observe and learn from the people around him. He figured out how mental hospitals work and how psychiatrists think, what they were looking for. He told them what they wanted to hear. He knew—even when his mental condition deteriorated—how to convince psychiatrists that he was sane. That way, he thought, they would release him. Meach considered himself an exceptional person who shouldn't be bound by the rules governing others, but he understood he needed to convince hospital staff that he felt otherwise. If they knew how he really felt, he might never be free.

In 1980 the California hospital was facing budget cuts and started sending prisoners like Meach back to their home states. He was transferred to the Alaska Psychiatric Institute in Anchorage. The Atascadero doctors warned API that Meach would remain stable only if held in a structured environment, kept on a steady dosage of Thorazine, an anti-psychotic drug, and kept away from alcohol. The psychiatrists said Meach admitted dreaming of killing all the women at Atascadero and fantasized about getting a gun and looking for a couple in a park, raping the girl and killing the man.

At API, Meach used what he had learned at Atascadero about manipulating the mental health system. Some members of the Alaska facility's staff came to see him as one of the sanest patients in the hospital, though in April 1981 one doctor noted that Meach's control over aggression seemed fragile. Several employees reported he seemed like a normal human being to them. Meach had unusual verbal skills and could more than hold his own in most discussions; one API worker said Meach could easily best anyone who chose to debate with him.

Since his disease seemed to be in remission—and since the hospital's mission was to return patients to society when they were deemed able to cope and no longer dangerous—Meach's Thorazine dosage was gradually reduced over a two-year test period. He was watched for signs of deterioration, but none were noticed.

Opinions about Meach's sanity were not unanimous. Dr. Mason Robison, superintendent of API, had visited Meach at Atascadero before his transfer to Anchorage and found him psychotic, aggressive when his medicine was reduced, and subconsciously fearful of increased freedom. In 1977 Robison wrote that Meach's "control is marginal at all times. It is my opinion he is likely to reoffend if he were not in a secure setting at this time."

In April 1981, two months before his scheduled retirement, Robison recommended that patient Meach be transferred to a more secure ward than the semi-secure wing in which he was housed. He said he felt Meach was "the most dangerous patient in the hospital, perhaps in the state of Alaska." Robison said Meach had delusions of grandeur, heard voices and music, and thought he was better than other people. Robison later testified that his experience and intuition caused him to believe Meach was more dangerous than he appeared. "My guiding principle is that if someone has killed a (stranger) in the past, then that person is dangerous forever."

Robison's recommendations somehow did not reach—or were ignored by—the professionals who would decide when and under what conditions Meach might be returned to society. While restrictions on his freedom were gradually eased, he was allowed to take his anti-psychotic medicine when he felt he needed it. Eventually he stopped taking the Thorazine altogether.

In late 1981 API began granting him unescorted leave privileges for up to six hours a day. The thought was that this leave would enable him to get a job, resume his long-abandoned college classes, and begin gradual readmission to community life. If he continued doing well, he was to be freed in June. When his daily leaves were lengthened to ten hours a day, he applied for and got a part-time job in Sears' clothing department.

Meach scored well on an intelligence and personality test given to all Sears employees. He got a ninety-nine; the average for most employees was in the sixties. He scored high in dominance, considered a leadership trait, and ranked near the top of the scale in emotional stability. Meach was good with customers and sometimes recited poetry to them. He did well in courses at the University of Alaska Anchorage in computer programming, accounting, and business. Though he was outwardly friendly, other students tended to shy away from anything more than casual conversation with him. They found his behavior odd, and he was too intense.

Meach went on occasional dates, and he opened an account at Merrill-Lynch so he could play the stock market. He started collecting dishes and household items for an apartment he would rent when he finally won his freedom. He joined Alcoholics Anonymous and took a second job as bookkeeper for a family grocery store on East Sixth Avenue. He did his job well, was reliable and generally friendly. His employers knew Meach was a mental patient; API staff told them his problems were alcohol- and drug-related. His keepers did not tell them that he was confined because he had killed a man in 1973, a man he had never met.

Meach showed his weird side selectively. An attractive elementary school teacher responded to his conversational efforts while running on the university's indoor track. After following her around the oval several times, Meach compared the thrill of running to the excitement of robbing a bank or raping a woman. "But I never robbed a bank," he puffed. "What about the other?" the teacher asked. She said Meach simply paused and smiled at her. She felt uncomfortable and walked hurriedly away.

Then Meach saw a chef at the Golden Lion Restaurant give a waitress a hug and call her "babe." When he tried to do the same thing, the woman became upset, which confused him. "I said that I had been there quite a while and would she like to hug me, put her arms around me," he said. "I wouldn't have minded it at all, to be one of the gang."

By late spring of 1982, Meach had resumed drinking and purchased two pistols, a .38 caliber weapon he named The Consumer and a .41 he named Mitch Toughie. He carried at least one whenever he felt threatened, hiding them near the API grounds when it was time to check back into the hospital. He bought the guns through a classified newspaper ad, but still needed ammunition. Buying bullets at a gun store would require that he show identification, and his ID card showed his home as 2900 Providence Drive, the address for Alaska Psychiatric Institute. Meach gave someone twenty dollars to buy ammunition for him.

Then he went to The Bicycle Shop and bought a new ten-speed Schwinn, a fancy bike with many accessories and a seat tall enough for his six-foot-six body. He haggled over the price until the clerk gave him fifteen dollars off.

On Monday, May 3, Meach was having a bad day. He had tried to call Michigan to check on his father, who was having a hip operation, but he couldn't get through. Someone had stolen his favorite shirt and a cassette tape. He tried to visit a woman but she refused to answer the door. Then he bought a topless dancer a ten-dollar glass of champagne, but he touched her several times and the woman got mad and refused to sit with him. His pending release from API was just a month away, but he was convinced that it would never happen, that he would spend the rest of his life in a loony bin.

"I didn't believe that the best I could do would ever be good enough," he said later. The district attorney's office was balking at his release and the API doctors were growing edgy.

During his bike travels through Anchorage, Meach had seen a small blue tent pitched in Russian Jack Springs Park, three hundred acres of popular greenery in East Anchorage. He peeked into the unoccupied tent and saw a hatchet and a knife. He was convinced that the tent also contained at least one cassette tape, perhaps more, to replace the tape stolen from him. Meach was angry and drunk that day, so he went to his hiding place, retrieved The Consumer, and headed for the tent, intending to steal something. Around 8:00 p.m. he rode his bike through the south end of the park, hid it in the woods, and made his way down an incline to the campsite.

A young welder spotted the hidden bicycle while walking through the park with his wife and two pit bulls. Because it was so carefully hidden, the welder assumed that the bike was stolen. He checked it out carefully, noting that it had an extra-large frame, a bell, a cable lock, an extended seat, and a blue cargo pouch containing a new blue shirt still in its wrapping. He was thinking of pushing the bike down to the road, where its owner might find it, when he saw a man peering at him from the woods.

"All of a sudden he just appeared at the edge of the woods," the welder said. "He was just sort of peeking out of the trees, like he wanted to be able to watch us without us seeing him." Thoroughly spooked, the young man dropped the bike, jumped into his van behind his wife and dogs, and drove off quickly. Meach headed down the incline to the waiting tent.

About ten minutes later the young welder began to wonder if the man in the woods was really the bike's owner. He drove back to the park and saw that the bike was gone and that an orange car was in the parking area. He looked down into the woods and saw several people lying on the ground. "I didn't go down there," he said. "I figured they were just lounging around in the grass, or maybe reading or something."

The young man looked around to make sure the weirdo who peered at him was gone. The only person he saw was a jogger coming down the bike path. "He was running super-quick, and when he saw me he really picked up the pace."

Dean Kimler and V. J. Sylvester had been living in the little blue tent ever since the advent of warm spring nights enabled them to move out of the back of Dean's Datsun station wagon. Both nineteen, they were unemployed and looking for work. Living the rugged life for a while seemed preferable to staying in crowded apartments, paying rent they couldn't really afford. V. J. was in love with sixteen-year-old Sabrina Imlach and had brought her to meet his family in North Kenai on Valentine's Day. Dean, V. J.'s buddy, had come with them.

They were driving around town on a warm spring night with Sabrina and her friend, Rebecca Phillips, also sixteen. The evening was cool and the boys were lightly dressed, so they decided to stop by the tent and pick up their jackets. They parked Dean's orange Datsun at the edge of the park. Dean ran ahead to grab the jackets and the others followed behind. When Dean reached the tent, he found Meach standing near it, looking suspicious. Dean asked Meach what he was doing there, then reached into the tent and pulled out two jackets and a paperback book, which Meach mistook for a cassette tape. Dean rose and walked past Meach to return to his friends, who were then approaching. Meach pulled the pistol from his pocket, raised it to eye level, and shot Dean in the back of the head. V. J. was then coming up the trail, heard the shot, and saw his friend fall. He instinctively ran toward Dean. As V. J. passed the towering stranger, Meach raised the pistol again and shot him in the face.

Running behind V. J. were Sabrina and Rebecca. When Sabrina approached, Meach held the pistol eight inches from her face and shot her between the eyes. In shock and fear, Rebecca approached and covered her face with her hand. Meach placed the gun against the webbing of her hand and shot through it into her brain. Dean and Sabrina died on the spot; V. J. and Rebecca never regained consciousness and died shortly afterward in hospital emergency wards.

Many people heard the shots, but most assumed they were firecrackers. Amy Hunsucker, a fifteen-year-old girl walking with two adults and her nine-year-old nephew, said the boy heard the sounds and shouted jokingly "Don't shoot! I surrender!" Moments later they encountered Charles Meach on the trail. The tall, balding man shouted "Get out of here" and shook his fists in the air. Investigators suspect Meach decided against shooting the four of them because The Consumer was down to just two bullets.

On the street above, the young welder drove up too late to hear the shots. To his eyes, the young people lying in the grass were simply lounging there. He was startled when the jogger, a man named James Carrington, ran by him with what appeared to be fear on his face. Carrington looked the welder in the eye, then put his running pace into high gear. The welder later realized

Carrington had seen the bodies and may have thought he was the murderer.

Since the fancy bicycle was now missing, the welder assumed there was nothing more he could do there and climbed back into his van to head home. Later his wife heard about the murders from a man at a gas station. She was terrified and told her husband, who was convinced they had seen the killer peering at them from the trees. They returned to the park, where police were combing the scene for clues. The welder told them about the new bicycle he had seen and the weird man who had stared at him. Carrington, the terrified jogger, told them he had encountered a tall man pushing a bicycle along a muddy ski trail. The cyclist greeted him cordially and went on. He described the cyclist as an adult white male in his late twenties.

Meach returned The Consumer to its hiding place and stopped by Anchorage Community College to wash his hands and remove any evidence that he had fired a gun. Then he went home to Alaska Psychiatric Hospital, checking in well before his scheduled curfew. That evening he watched a television news report about the murders. A nurse who watched the report with him said Meach seemed normal and had no particular reaction to the murders.

His boss, Janet Patrick, said that when Meach returned to work at the grocery store two days later, he seemed happy. "I was glad to see him feeling good," she said. "He asked me if I'd heard about the murders. I said it was such a waste of young life. I hope they catch him and take him out and hang him," she commented. Meach scowled, then became quiet.

The community was shocked by the enormity of the killings: the murder of four innocent young people enjoying themselves in a city park on a quiet spring evening. Though a double murder and suicide the same night were also taxing their resources, the Anchorage Police Department assigned every available officer to the investigation. At one point twenty-five investigators were working the case. They found few clues at the scene pointing directly to any suspect, but dozens of people had been in the park that night—people who were jogging, walking on trails, or playing softball. Many told the investigators everything they could remember that seemed suspicious. One young man who had once dated one of the dead girls was brought in for questioning on the basis of a tip from the girl's relatives. Detectives quickly ruled him out as a suspect.

The most intriguing leads were those from the young welder and the jogger, both of whom had seen the bicycle and its rider. The young man proved to have a phenomenal memory and gave investigators a detailed description of the fancy bike and its accessories.

Detectives Tim Casper and Mike Redding called on Mike Sanderson, manager of The Bicycle Shop, the local Schwinn dealer. Sanderson remembered selling a bike just like the one the young welder described. The buyer had been a tall man who needed a twenty-seven-inch frame, a relatively rare size. Sanderson had shown the man a ten-speed that was just his size.

"He told me he'd buy it if I fixed him up with a handlebar bag on the front, and a lock and a cable," the manager said. "And the last thing he wanted was a ding-dong bell, something to warn people that you're coming. That's what really helped me remember who he was."

Sanderson pulled his records and told the detectives the man lived at 2900 Providence Drive, the address of the psychiatric hospital. The man's name was listed as Charles Meach. Casper and Redding talked to Meach at the hospital, but he denied being at Russian Jack Springs on Monday night. He was adamant about that claim and refused to tell the investigators why he was confined. They ran a computer check on Meach's record, which showed nothing, but a query to state archives at Juneau brought details of the 1973 murder conviction.

The officers again talked to Meach and took his photo. Meach asked them about Ralph Christianson, the detective to whom he had confessed the grocery bagger murder. Told that Christianson was now a captain, Meach gave the investigators a poem he had written about Jesus and asked them to give it to the captain. The officers left and Meach returned to his room.

On Thursday, three days after the murders, API staff psychiatrist David Coons interviewed his patient. Meach mentioned that he had been near the park when the shooting started, but said he "vamoosed" when he heard the shots. He said he had been drinking and was afraid his pass would be revoked if the API staff heard about it. After a time Meach blurted out that he had, in fact, killed the four youngsters. Dr. Coons said that when Meach admitted the murders, "I was really shook."

Coons contacted the two detectives, who immediately called Christianson because of his previous connection with Meach, asking him to come to the hospital. The captain once again sat across a table from Charles Meach and once again heard him confess to murder, this time of four people. "This is the second time we've talked like this," Meach commented. He was placed in a lineup at police headquarters. He and five police officers all wore identical blue uniforms. Four out of six people who had been at the park that night identified him.

The trial was moved to Fairbanks because the judge felt the Anchorage community had been too traumatized by the crime to find an uninformed and unbiased jury. During one interview, Meach asked a psychiatrist whether he should act crazy during the court proceedings to help convince the jury that he was insane. Meach went to trial the following December, attempted unsuccessfully to plead innocent by reason of insanity, and was found guilty on four counts of first-degree murder two days after Christmas. He was sentenced to 396 years in prison, with the provision that he be treated as needed for his mental illness.

Found among Meach's belongings in his API room was a novel by mystery writer John D. MacDonald, *On Monday We Killed Them All.*

Assistant District Attorney Larry Weeks, who had earlier tried to block Meach's release from API, defended the hospital for its decision to allow the patient unsupervised leave. "Here's a guy who was basically in for ten years," he said, "and there were independent psychiatric exams done on him by people from outside the institution, and it was reviewed by the court. Lots of people go to jail for murder and they don't serve ten years." The victims' families sued API for giving passes to a dangerous patient. The hospital settled out of court, paying each family $150,000.

Just months after the murders, the Alaska Legislature passed a law that put an end to the claim of innocence by reason of insanity as a valid defense. Offenders in any such future cases might be sent to mental hospitals for treatment, but they would still be required to serve their prison terms when released from psychiatric facilities.

chapter three

THE CARIBOU MURDERS

The people of Kiana in northwest Alaska were shocked and angered by the cold-blooded murder of three Eskimo hunters. The killer's shockingly short confinement in prison further angered the village.

Why Norman Johnson shot his three Eskimo hosts may never be known. What is known is that the three men took the young man along on a caribou-hunting trip at the request of his father while the temperature sat at 50 below zero. Butch Johnson, as Norman was known, was found two days later, hiking down the frozen Kobuk River. He said an unknown man had motored into their remote camp after dark, argued with the three Eskimo men, then killed them. Johnson said he had escaped by crawling under the tent wall and hiding behind a tree while the gunman poured bullets into his friends.

Death was no stranger in the arctic village of Kiana, in far northwestern Alaska, but nobody could ever remember there being a homicide. The Eskimos are a non-violent people, and a triple murder was unthinkable.

The only survivor was this twenty-year-old white man from the far-off city of Anchorage, one whose story was quite suspicious, and the victims were three well-known local people. Many of the villagers were related to one another and to the three murdered men.

Alaska State Troopers sent an officer from Kotzebue to investigate. He found that tensions and emotions in Kiana were running high, threats were being muttered, and white teachers at the Bureau of Indian Affairs School were asking to leave. The officer's supervisor decided that Trooper Lorry Schuerch, an officer with Eskimo heritage, should be brought in to assist. Schuerch had been born in Kiana, was related to many of the villagers, and knew the others quite well. One of the victims was a close friend of his.

The arctic hunting camp was an alien and hostile place for Butch Johnson, who had only recently moved to Anchorage from his native state of California. His father was a carpenter who moved from job to job in California, each time bringing his family with him. The frequent moves disrupted Butch's education. He was rarely in trouble but tested low in intelligence and was disinterested in school, dropping out at age sixteen. Butch worked at a variety of jobs, all for short periods, and followed his parents to Alaska when his father moved there to take advantage of a booming construction industry. He had no luck finding a job to his liking and decided to resume his education. He began working for a high school equivalency certificate at Anchorage Community College.

Butch's lackluster school and work performance left him with low self-esteem. His father felt a wilderness hunting trip might increase his son's self-confidence and bolster his lagging morale. Butch had hunted rabbits and doves in California, so his father felt a big game expedition in the Arctic might be just the ticket.

Butch's main present at Christmas in 1969 was his first rifle, a lever-action Winchester 30-30. The second half of the present was an invitation to come north to Kiana, where his dad was on temporary assignment as a supervisor constructing low-income state housing. The homes were being built under a unique sweat-equity program in which the people of the village helped erect their own houses without pay.

Butch had great misgivings about the caribou hunt. He considered Anchorage itself a cold and alien place, compared with California, and distant Kiana in the deep-freeze part of Alaska held little attraction for him. He was intimidated by the idea of the hunt but agreed to go to please his father, and he tried to seem enthusiastic.

Freddie Jackson was a forty-three-year-old Inupiat Eskimo, one of the few paid workers on the housing project in Kiana. His boss, Al Johnson, prevailed on Freddie to take Butch hunting when his son came up from Anchorage in late January. Freddie agreed and arranged with two friends, Clarence Arnold, thirty-nine, from Kotzebue, and Oscar Henry Sr., sixty-four, of Kiana, to run their snowmachines up the Kobuk River, set up a tent camp, and hunt with them when Freddie arrived with Butch.

The weather was horrendous: 50 below zero, with no wind, and dense ice fog in low-lying areas. Most people who had a choice stayed indoors, putting off travel and hunting trips until the weather improved. The people of the Arctic know how to dress and function in extreme weather. Hunting in such conditions was entirely possible, could be done quite comfortably, but traveling in deep cold could be unpleasant and keeping machinery working was often a downright nuisance. It would have been a good time to find things to do indoors, near the fire, but Freddie Jackson had promised his boss, and both Clarence and Oscar were willing to go and ready for an adventure, as always.

Kiana was then a village of about three hundred people just north of the Arctic Circle. In January it was just emerging from the depths of winter, the December days when the sun shone for less than three hours and hugged the horizon the entire time, throwing little light and no heat. But now the sun was up before noon and stayed above the tundra until late afternoon. Though spring was still but a distant dream, the lengthening days meant its ultimate victory over the penetrating cold was now assured; the men were restless and eager to go afield. And since Butch was scheduled to fly home in a few days, the window of opportunity for a hunting trip was fairly narrow.

Clarence and Oscar climbed on their snowmachines on the morning of Friday, January 23, and headed up the thick ice of the Kobuk River, their gear-laden sleds trailing behind. They traveled sixty-five miles upriver and pitched their white canvas tent on the river's north shore. They settled in, built a fire in the woodstove, put water on to heat and set up bunks, then fixed a meal, worked on their equipment, and waited for Freddie and Butch to arrive.

In Kiana, Butch was outfitted for arctic travel with plenty of warm clothing, including a pair of caribou hide mukluks—Eskimo boots—made for him by an Eskimo family that had befriended Al Johnson and helped him prepare for his son's midwinter visit. Since Freddie had access to only one snowmachine, Butch was forced to ride in the sled towed behind Freddie's Arctic Cat. The sled had no suspension and Butch had to hold on tight to avoid being pitched out, all the while being sprayed by snow thrown up from Freddie's spinning tracks. The travel accommodations posed no particular risk but made for an uncomfortable trip.

They left Kiana at 1:00 p.m. and reached camp in late afternoon, with Butch sliding doggedly along behind. The four hunted briefly, then settled into camp, ate dinner, and climbed into their bunks. Next morning the Eskimos climbed on their machines and headed off, with Butch riding once again in Freddie's sled. A few miles from their tent, the hunters spotted a small caribou herd and sped off to get into shooting position before the animals ran away.

While Butch had been able to hang on and stay in the sled along the relatively flat river, doing the same while racing overland proved to be something entirely different. Early in the chase Butch reached for his rifle, lost his grip, and went flying out of the sled. Freddie roared away, afraid that if he stopped to pick up Butch he would lose the caribou and a chance to lay in a supply of fresh meat. He planned to return for him after downing the animals, but young Johnson walked up to the kill site while the Eskimos were still dressing the fallen caribou.

Butch was furious and panting, his labored breath freezing in the enveloping cold and falling as frost. Throughout his frantic hike, Butch had wondered whether the men intended to return for him at all. He didn't know them well and couldn't be sure they hadn't planned to let him freeze to death out there.

Butch unenthusiastically helped dress out the downed caribou. He had never worked on a newly dead large animal and found the experience disturbing, but it seemed the only way to get back to camp and the woodstove as quickly as possible. He watched in disgust as one of his companions slit open a female caribou, exposing an unborn calf inside. His companions were experienced subsistence hunters and wondered at his inexperience and ineptness, but finished their work in relative silence.

When the party headed back to camp, Clarence Arnold's machine refused to start in the cold, so he walked the mile back to the tent. Upon arriving, he told his fellow hunters he had seen snowmachine lights on the river. Shortly afterward Clarence Wood, a thirty-two-year-old Eskimo neighbor from Ambler, motored into camp to say hello, warm up, and have a cup of coffee. Wood was running upriver to Ambler after his weekly trip to Kiana and was checking on friends' cabins and camps along the way. The hunters invited him to stay for caribou soup. He noticed that the three hunters were hard at work on their day's kill, working on their snowmachines, hauling ice for water, and cutting wood for the stove. Butch Johnson was nowhere in sight.

Wood first saw Butch sitting on a food box inside the tent. One of the men asked him to move and Butch moved sullenly to his bunk, saying not two words while the visitor was in camp. Since Oscar Henry spoke little English and all four of the men felt more comfortable speaking Eskimo, they told Butch they would be conversing in their native language. They told him not to worry, that they would not be talking about him, then began laughing and talking as old friends do. At one point the hunters did tell their visitor about Butch's misadventure in falling out of the sled, but Wood said Butch knew what they were talking about and didn't react. After dinner, Wood climbed back on his snowmachine and headed upriver again, leaving the four hunters to the quiet of the wilderness.

"The only thing unusual I noted about their camp," Wood said later, "was the fact that the boy didn't even attempt to help with the work. No one said anything about it, but I had the feeling that they would have felt a little better if the boy would at least make an attempt to help."

On Sunday afternoon, pilot Harold Lie and Dr. Ray Lang were hunting wolves in Lie's two-seater SuperCub and flying along a snowmachine trail near the Kobuk Sand Dunes when Lie spotted a wolf in the middle of the trail. "Get ready," he shouted, and swung open the top half of the airplane's door.

Dr. Lang gripped his shotgun and peered ahead over the pilot's shoulder. As they approached, he slipped the muzzle out into the super-cold windstream. Suddenly the creature below stood up and held its arms up straight, appearing to surrender, then fell down.

"Wait!" Lie shouted. "It's a man."

Below them a haggard-looking Butch Johnson waved furiously, afraid he would be shot, though not just because he looked like a wild animal. Lie made a quick circle and set his plane's skis down on the snow. Butch ran to the plane as it stopped. The two fliers were startled by the young man's appearance. His clothes were spattered with blood; he told them he had been running all night and day since a stranger invaded their hunting camp, argued with his Eskimo friends, and killed all three. He had escaped with his life but was afraid the killer might still be stalking him.

The fliers loaded Butch into the SuperCub, putting him in the lone seat behind the pilot. Dr. Lang folded himself into the cargo area, his knees wedged on each side of Butch's shoulders. Harold Lie was troubled by the survivor's story, felt it didn't ring true. Butch fell asleep as soon as the SuperCub's skis left the snow. Lie reached surreptitiously into his survival gear bag, pulled out a hatchet, and stashed it near his aircraft's control stick, just in case.

Minutes later the Public Health Service radio operator at Kiana received a call from the SuperCub reporting that it had rescued a man who claimed he had witnessed three murders. The radio operator relayed the message to the State Trooper office in Kotzebue, a larger community forty miles southwest of Kiana. The fliers dropped the survivor off at Kiana, where he was turned over to a public health nurse, checked over, and put to bed. Harold Lie then recruited a friend and flew back upriver to buzz the hunting camp. They spotted one body lying outside the tent but could see no other sign of life. It was growing too dark to land, so they headed back to Kiana.

In Kotzebue, Trooper Bob Boatright called Shellabarger Flying Service and chartered an aircraft, then recruited Kotzebue Police Chief William Stevens to come with him. They flew over the hunting camp but were unable to land, so they too headed downriver and landed at Kiana. There they found a community in shock over reports of an unbelievable triple homicide. The only survivor was a white boy whose story seemed unlikely. Kiana was swept by rumors, which quickly reached the town's small white community.

When the school superintendent requested permission to remove his white teachers from Kiana, the state decided to call in Trooper Lorenz "Lorry" Schuerch, Alaska's first part-Eskimo trooper, who was then working traffic detail in Fairbanks. The State Troopers had long had Alaska Native officers, some from Southcentral and Southeast Alaska. Their success demonstrated that officers with local knowledge and rapport in Native communities sometimes had an advantage over non-Native troopers, especially in delicate situations. Lorry Schuerch had been a State Trooper for two years and had special credentials for an investigation in Kiana; he was part Inupiat Eskimo and was born in the village, where his father owned the trading post and his brother was mayor. Victim Freddie Jackson had been one of his close friends.

Schuerch hopped on the first jet to Kotzebue and caught a connector flight to Kiana. He reported to Boatright, who was interviewing witnesses, and began working with a search party preparing to follow Butch Johnson's trail back to the hunting camp. The searchers were asked to see what they could find and help collect evidence at the murder scene, then break down the camp and retrieve the victims' personal gear.

When Trooper Boatright interviewed Butch Johnson that afternoon, Johnson said he had gotten a good look at the gunman who killed his companions and was positive he would recognize the shooter if he saw him again. Boatright wrote in his report that Johson told him the gunman "was about five-foot-nine, kind of fat, wearing a dark blue Comfy hip-length parka with a light-colored wolf ruff. He had brown, down-filled Army-type trousers with zippers in the legs, dark store-boughten snow boots with rubber soles and cloth tops, and wearing a black earband with the word 'Alaska' written across it.

"He was driving a yellow snowmachine pulling a cargo-type sled that was filled. There was a canvas across the load, and I don't know what was in it. I was in my sleeping bag in the back of the tent, and he and the other

Eskimos were talking in the front of the tent. I guess they started arguing, as they were raising their voices.

"This guy that was visiting got up and left the tent, and we turned out the lamps. He started his machine and then it died. . . . Shortly after it stopped, there was a bunch of shots and one of the men with me hollered 'No, no', and I guess he took one of the first shots, as he fell partway across me. I slipped out of my sleeping bag and out the back of the tent and ran back a short distance and hid behind a tree. The guy kept firing and firing, both small and large caliber, and then all was quiet.

"I saw the fellow walk up to the tent, do something inside, and then come out again. He looked around for a while, then got on his machine and left, heading toward Kiana. I stayed put until the sound of his machine became faint, and then I went to the back of the tent. . . . Everyone was dead."

Johnson told Trooper Boatright that he tried unsuccessfully to start one of the snowmachines, then ran off down the trail unarmed. "I didn't want to stick around because I was afraid the guy might come after me."

Butch Johnson's description of the killer sounded a lot like Clarence Wood, but Johnson said he had met Wood when the man came through camp and Wood was definitely not the killer. Boatright advised Johnson that he himself was a suspect and recommended that he and his father leave the village as quickly as possible. Both departed within the hour for Kotzebue and then Anchorage, where they were met by another state trooper and given instructions on when and where to appear for further interviews.

One of Trooper Schuerch's first priorities was to try to calm the community down. His presence helped, since he was one of them, providing assurance that justice would be done. Schuerch made several visits and then dropped by the home of Paul Henry, son of murder victim Oscar Henry. Paul was reportedly drinking and had threatened to shoot every white man in the village; his threats had been a principal concern among both whites and Eskimos in Kiana. Schuerch found the man sitting at his kitchen table, a bottle in front of him, still angry but quite sober. Schuerch was Paul's second cousin and had known him for years. Schuerch later recounted the discussion in an interview.

"Mind if I have a drink," the trooper said, taking a seat.

Paul poured him one and handed it across the table. Schuerch sipped his drink as he gave his cousin a low-key lecture, warning him about making threats. Schuerch told Paul that he could wind up in jail, especially if he shot anyone.

"I don't care!" Paul responded, pain in his voice.

"I want your rifles!" Schuerch demanded.

"You don't have a warrant."

"I'm not talking as a trooper," Schuerch said. "I'm talking as your cousin. Give me your rifles!"

The man complied and Schuerch took the guns to one of Paul Henry's relatives in another part of town. He asked that the rifles be returned only after Paul calmed down. That family showdown reduced the tension level markedly and the villagers turned away from thoughts of revenge and back toward dealing with their shock and grief.

Boatright flew to the murder scene next morning with Chief Stevens from Kotzebue, Kiana Mayor Vincent Schuerch, a helper, and a pilot. The aircraft landed upriver from the camp, then took off and circled while the two police officers approached on foot. Boatright and Stevens would deal with the killer, if he was still in the area, and those above watched to see if anyone tried to flee. Finding nothing except the three dead Eskimos and their gear, the officers radioed for the plane to land and began their investigation.

Freddie Jackson lay in front of the tent, his hands grasping the ends of a pine bough, the middle portion of the bough firmly clenched between his teeth. He had been shot and had apparently walked or crawled out of the tent and bit down on the stick to ease his pain, then was finished off with one or more bullets. Beneath Freddie's body was a thick pool of blood extending down through the snow to the tundra below, suggesting that his heart had been pumping long after he was shot.

The frozen bodies of Clarence Arnold and Oscar Henry lay inside the tent. Clarence had been shot repeatedly. Oscar had apparently been wounded while pulling on his heavy clothing, had fallen with his trousers still at half-mast, and then was finished off by someone who smashed his head with a rifle butt. All three bodies were frozen to the snow. Inside the coffeepot was a spent .243 slug, apparently stopped in place by water that had then drained out. The bloody bolt of a .243 rifle lay under a sleeping bag near Oscar's head.

Boatright hiked around the camp but could find no fresh snowmachine tracks except those left by the hunters and by Clarence Wood, their Ambler-bound visitor. He drew a map of the murder scene, logged the evidence, and authorized loading the bodies aboard the aircraft for shipment to Kiana and then on to Anchorage, where they would be autopsied.

When they returned to Kiana, Mayor Schuerch dispatched a thirteen-member search party to run up the river by snowmachine to the spot where Butch Johnson had been found, then follow his trail back to the murder scene. They were ordered to watch for evidence along the trail and signs of any other snowmachines traveling in the area. The party searched all day Tuesday until dark, then returned the next morning. No sign of unknown travelers turned up. But about a mile and a quarter from the hunting camp, one of the searchers saw where someone had left the trail, his tracks leading to a small mound in the snow. They brushed away the snow and found Freddie Jackson's Winchester .243, its bolt missing, its butt encrusted with blood. At the campsite, the search party gathered up the personal gear of the murder victims, including guns, sleeping bags, and clothing, and brought it back to Kiana.

Clarence Wood heard about the shootings on the radio and headed for Kiana immediately. He realized that police would want to talk to him. There he was interviewed by Boatright and gave the names of witnesses who had seen him the night of the murders, after he had left the hunting camp. Boatright and Trooper Schuerch questioned the witnesses and decided Wood was an unlikely suspect.

Butch Johnson was interviewed at his Anchorage home the morning after he and his father returned to the city. The story he told Trooper Investigator Dean Bivins differed significantly from what he had told Boatright. This time he said that when he and the hunters returned from chasing caribou on Saturday afternoon, they found a sleeping bag had disappeared and their belongings were strewn around the tent.

He told about Clarence Wood's arrival, his stay for dinner and departure. Then a second man arrived, argued with the Eskimo men, and started to leave. Johnson said he heard the man's snowmobile start as

they were preparing for bed; then the machine's engine died and bullets began tearing through the tent
walls. He said he had slipped away through the back
of the tent, and then heard his friends shouting when
the shooting stopped. He said he watched as the man
went back into the tent, then came out, climbed on
his snowmachine, and headed off toward Kiana.
Johnson said he went back to the tent, found everyone dead, and gathered up his clothes. He tried to start
one of the snowmachines but couldn't get it going
and finally ran off down the trail.

Two days later Butch Johnson was interviewed again
at trooper headquarters. Confronted with the accumulating evidence, he admitted he had killed his three companions. Johnson told Bivins he left the tent to go to the
bathroom, picked up the .243, and fired seven times
into the tent. When the gun ran out of bullets, he picked
up his own rifle and kept shooting. He could give no
reason for the murders. The autopsy showed Freddie had
been shot at least four times, Clarence had been shot
somewhere between three and six times, and Oscar had
been shot at least twice.

Lorry Schuerch went to the murder scene and
attempted to reconstruct the crime and pin down a
few discrepancies. He said it appeared Johnson had
shot his three companions, then headed down the trail
on foot, unaware that at least two were still alive.
When he heard Freddie Jackson trying to start a
snowmachine back at the camp, he ran back and shot
him again, then went into the tent and beat Oscar
Henry to death with the butt of Freddie's gun. The
.243 was empty at that point and Johnson failed to
notice that its bolt had fallen out.

Butch Johnson was tried in Anchorage in January 1971. Psychiatrist J. Ray Langdon, testifying on his behalf, said that at the time of the killings, Johnson "had what we would call a psychotic lapse; he was divorced from reality." Langdon said the shooting of the caribou made the site for him a massacre ground. "Norman was in a totally unfamiliar situation in the extremely cold arctic wilderness. . . . Norman was experiencing what was primarily a panic."

Barbara Ure, another psychiatrist testifying on Johnson's behalf, said: "He was already insecure as to who he was. Having lost contact with his culture and his geography, he was displaced. He had absolutely no preparation for this caribou hunt." She testified Johnson felt threatened by his Eskimo companions, who were speaking a language he didn't understand and didn't appear to like him. In his mind he was shooting them in self-defense, she said.

The trial judge denied Johnson's plea of temporary insanity and found him guilty of three counts of second-degree murder. The judge sentenced him to life in prison but ordered that he receive psychiatric treatment. The judge left it to the parole board to decide when he might be released.

Johnson served much of his time in a California prison, which offered better psychiatric care than was available in Alaska. He was freed on parole after four years and was discharged from parole in May 1986, on recommendation of his parole officer. An Alaska parole official said later that such an early discharge from parole is so rare that few prisoners even apply for it, but it was apparently considered justified because Johnson's behavior was exemplary both while in prison and on parole.

When word of Johnson's early release was later received in Kiana, the community was shocked anew by the crime they had found hard to believe and considered worthy of long imprisonment.

chapter four

BIRDMAN OF ALCATRAZ

Robert Stroud, later known as "the Birdman of Alcatraz," expected a prison term of two to three years for killing a Juneau man who had beaten the woman he loved. Stroud spent the next 54 years in jail.

Alaska's most famous criminal did not commit a notorious crime. Instead he shot a grifter whose death was a civic improvement. He turned himself in to the federal marshal at Juneau and was told by prosecutors he would probably get a sentence of two or three years—after all, there were many men with worse crimes running free in the territory. And the man he shot had beaten the woman Robert Stroud loved.

Stroud pled guilty to manslaughter, but it was his misfortune that he came before a reformist judge bent on reducing lawlessness in Alaska. The judge gave him the maximum, twelve years, and Stroud was shipped to the federal penitentiary at McNeil Island in Puget Sound, Washington. He never returned to Alaska, and his prison term eventually grew to encompass the balance of his life, fifty-four years, much of it in solitary confinement. He became the best-known prisoner in American history.

Stroud was at first angry, but grew pensive and thoughtful in his lonely cell, unleashing an imposing intellect. He built his third-grade education into the equivalent of a doctorate as he studied wild birds that fell into his exercise yard, then canaries in his cell. He became an authority on ornithology and wrote two authoritative books. His story was the subject of several books and a movie starring Burt Lancaster, *Birdman of Alcatraz*. Whether he was the rather saintly but tough man portrayed by Lancaster is an open question. Stroud was a troublesome prisoner and brought many of his problems on himself.

Robert Stroud was born in 1890 in Seattle to a woman battered by both of her husbands. Robbie was her third child and first son. She tried to shelter him from the wrath of his father, her second husband. She was not always successful; Robert's dad beat and abused him, sometimes threatening to kill him and everybody else in the family. Elizabeth Stroud was bitter and possessive. She hated beatings that passed that hatred on to Robbie, fanning it into an obsession in the boy. His rage flamed at both beatings and punishment, deserved or not.

Robbie's lack of social grace left him uneasy at school. He was tall and thin, and he was left-handed, which was considered abnormal. He sat apart from other children, was hesitant to raise his hand—even to go to the toilet—and ran home at recess. When his teachers complained, his father beat him. In the third grade, Robbie stopped going to school altogether.

When his father left economically depressed Seattle for the Klondike gold fields in 1900, ten-year-old Robbie became the male head of the family and the protector of his younger brother, Marc. He once drove off three boys who threatened to beat Marc, the boys fleeing before Robbie's ferocity. His father found no gold and returned to Seattle empty-handed. The family welcomed him reluctantly and he soon took up with a neighbor woman.

At age thirteen, young Robert ran away to become a hobo, riding the steel rods slung below freight trains. He returned at sixteen and went to work installing electrical fixtures. But he was fascinated by the idea of freedom, especially the freedom of the sea. He hung around Seattle's docks and befriended sailors, lumberjacks, and other transients.

Stroud heard about Alaska from friends just before a fight with his father. In May 1908, at age eighteen, he signed on with a section gang headed for Katalla to build a railroad. The section crews traveled in a slow and smelly converted cattle boat and were dropped at a rudimentary port on the eastern Gulf of Alaska. Stroud's crew worked for the Guggenheim Syndicate, one of two competing groups racing to build a railroad from the sea to a great copper strike in the Wrangell Mountains. When a storm washed out a breakwater and halted work, Stroud and his crew struck out for Cordova. They signed on with a rival team organized by the colorful young engineer Michael J. Heney, who had earlier built the White Pass & Yukon Railway into the Klondike gold fields.

Heney's men were sinking caissons 150 feet deep into roaring rivers and built a four-span bridge across the face of a glacier. Like the other workers, Stroud spent much of his free time in the twenty-six saloons lining Cordova's short main street, but his spiritual life was not entirely neglected. One of his favorite taverns, the Red Dragon, had an altar suspended from ropes below the ceiling. On Sundays it was lowered for church services, and a beer mug was passed for the collection.

The hard work took its toll on Stroud and a childhood bout with pneumonia recurred. Kitty O'Brien, a dance-hall girl and prostitute, nursed him back to health. Kitty was thirty-six—twice Robert's age—and had deep blue eyes, a clear complexion, and a strong, honest face. She also had one of the most beautiful figures in all Alaska. Robert and Kitty became roommates. Her feelings toward him were initially maternal, but his youthful passion soon made him her devoted lover. Stroud made money by selling popcorn from the back of a wagon. One day in September, one of his customers was an old acquaintance from Katalla, Charlie Dahmer, a nattily dressed bartender who had once been Kitty's lover. Their conversation is related by author Thomas E. Gaddis in *Birdman of Alcatraz:*

"Flip you double or nothing for a sack of that stuff," Dahmer said of the popcorn.

"I thought you were staying in Katalla," Stroud said. "Where you headed?"

"Juneau. Tending bar at the Montana. Look me up if you come down."

As winter approached, the popcorn trade grew quiet. Stroud sold the business, and in November he and Kitty boarded a boat for Juneau and found a room in the old Clarke Building. He looked for work, which was scarce. The town was filled with stranded miners. Most gambled and drank, spending their little gold on dance-hall women. Tempers grew short; shootouts and sickness sent many to Juneau's cemetery. But the bars and dance halls did a thriving business. Kitty took a job in a cabaret and tried to comfort Stroud, who grew morose and hung out with others living on borrowed cash and small hope.

Charlie Dahmer made money at the Montana bar, but lost it at the gaming tables. Dahmer invited Stroud to visit his cottage and urged him to bring Kitty. She was hesitant but agreed, telling Stroud to be careful. "I'm not afraid of him," Stroud said. "He's good company." Stroud said Dahmer owed him a few dollars and was unlikely to pay, so they might as well get his money's worth by drinking Charlie's liquor.

Stroud and Kitty spent an enjoyable evening with Charlie and his roommate Nels. Everyone toasted Kitty, and Dahmer kept his eyes on her. Stroud and Kitty came back on January 18, 1909, and Charlie broke out a cache of beer he had liberated from the Montana saloon. Early in the evening, Stroud headed to the Juneau dock for a sack of fish to add to Dahmer's table.

When he returned he found the cottage empty. A chair was upended and Charlie's bunk was torn up. Stroud ran back to his room, where Kitty lay groaning on their bed. Her eyes were blackened and a red line circled her neck where Dahmer had torn off a gold chain and locket containing a picture of her daughter. Kitty told Stroud that Dahmer had said he would keep the locket until she came to stay with him.

Stroud poured her a large glass of whiskey. Kitty sipped it and mumbled angrily, "Kill the beast, kill him, kill him."

Stroud opened a drawer and pulled out Kitty's old .38 single-action revolver. He flipped open the barrel and saw the gun was empty, then rummaged through the drawer looking for bullets. There were none. "No," Kitty cried from the bed. "I didn't mean it—no, don't go back there. He'll kill you!"

Stroud put the gun back in the drawer and slammed it shut. He sat stroking her hair, remembering the times his mother had sat weeping after beatings from his drunken father. Rage swelled up in him, a rage like none before. He took the gun and stopped at the Jorgensen store to buy a box of cartridges, then headed for Dahmer's cottage.

Charlie returned and struck a match to light his lamp, then was startled to see Stroud sitting quietly in a corner. "Did you beat Kitty?" Stroud demanded.

"Why no, Bob," he said. "Kitty fell down. We were drinking." Dahmer edged closer to Stroud. "Stay there," Stroud shouted. "Let's have Kitty's locket and that money you owe me."

Dahmer tried to tackle Stroud, who pulled out the gun and fired. The shot missed and Dahmer kept charging. Stroud fired again, but Dahmer kept coming. Stroud slammed the gun against Dahmer's head and the man crashed to the floor. Dahmer tried to rise, and fell back dead. The second bullet had penetrated his right temple and driven down into his pelvis.

As he left, Stroud encountered one of Dahmer's neighbors, who asked, "What's the matter in there?"

"Nothing," Stroud said. He hurried home, returned the pistol to the dresser drawer, and placed his remaining bullets beside it. He slipped the locket and broken chain into the sleeping Kitty's stocking. Five minutes later he entered the Juneau City Marshal's office and announced, "I shot a man." Stroud was taken to the federal jail and placed in a cell for the first time in his life.

Stroud told Marshal Herbert Faulkner that he and Dahmer had argued over money, omitting any mention of Kitty's beating. That omission led many in Juneau to speculate that Stroud had been Kitty's pimp and that Dahmer had tried to short-change him, leading to the fatal argument. At first Kitty told the marshal she had urged Stroud to kill Dahmer, then recanted and claimed she had been distraught and didn't know what she was saying. Faulkner arrested her as well, charging both with first-degree murder.

Stroud's lawyer, T. J. Lyons, fought to move the trial to Skagway. He claimed that heavy press coverage of the shooting would bias any jury in Juneau. Dahmer was a well-known bartender and Stroud was new in town and associated with a known prostitute. The *Alaska Dispatch* speculated that Stroud had pistol-whipped the bartender and shot him as he lay unconscious. Lyons gathered affidavits from prominent Juneau residents saying that feelings in the town were "very bitter" against Stroud.

Lyons was a distinguished Juneau lawyer hired by Stroud's mother to defend her son. Unfortunately for Stroud, Lyons was appointed to a federal judgeship shortly before the trial. His replacement lawyer suggested he plead guilty to manslaughter, which then carried a minimum penalty of one year. The lawyer told Stroud he would probably get two to three years. One aspect of such a plea held great attraction to the young lover. His admission of guilt to manslaughter meant the charges against Kitty would most likely be dropped.

Lyons' defensive move got Stroud away from the angry crowd in Juneau and resulted in Kitty's release, but it placed Stroud right before the Skagway bench of new federal judge E. E. Cushman, who arrived from the States determined to crack down on lawlessness in the Alaska Territory. Stroud was his first case. Cushman accepted the manslaughter plea, freed Kitty, and threw the book at Stroud, giving him the statutory limit of twelve years in the federal penitentiary at McNeil Island.

Stroud last saw Alaska from the porthole of the brig on the SS *Jefferson* in September 1909. He was nineteen years old. Most of his fellow passengers, those not in the brig, were celebrants en route to the Alaska-Yukon-Pacific Exposition in Seattle.

McNeil Island was a stern prison and Stroud proved a sullen and angry prisoner. He considered himself and his fellow prisoners to be underdogs in a gray brotherhood. At McNeil, Stroud grew into a man. Author Thomas E. Gaddis described him as "six-foot-three, rail thin, taciturn and withdrawn, with eyes as hard as a blue china plate." Kitty wrote each week, her letters assuring that she loved only him. After a year, she visited him in prison. Gaddis tells how she was shocked by his sullen appearance, he by the damage to her face and figure by excess food and liquor.

"Glad you came, Kitty."

"Bob, you're different. Your eyes make me feel miles off." She blinked rapidly. "Bob, have you forgot your old Kitty?"

"No. Your letters mean a lot inside this joint."

"I'll write as long as you're here."

Shortly after the visit, Kitty's letters stopped. He was heartbroken and confused, learning only years later that his family had asked the warden to block her letters. They blamed Kitty for the shooting and for Robert's fate.

Stroud was working in the prison kitchen and was seen stealing food, which he brought back for his cellmate. Another prisoner reported the theft, trading the information for better treatment. The informant testified at Stroud's parole hearing, resulting in parole being denied. Stroud was furious, started a fight, and drove a paring knife into the man's shoulder. He lost all privileges and had six months added to his sentence, raising the possibility that he would remain imprisoned past age thirty.

When a new cell house opened at the maximum security prison at Leavenworth, Kansas, in 1912, other federal prisons were invited to send their hardest cases. McNeil Island won fifty slots and Washington prison officials included Robert Stroud in their allocation. At Leavenworth, Stroud's cellmate was a young safecracker named Eddie, who told tales of the great prison break of 1910, when convicts rammed a locomotive through the under-construction prison gate. He told of cruel guards, of men beaten to death or chained to a twenty-five-pound iron ball, which they had to carry to move about. Stroud told Eddie he would never let himself be beaten by anyone, ever again. He wrote to his mother, referring to convicts as "my own people."

Despite Stroud's growing hatred, his mind began to expand in a way he had never experienced before. When the warden toured Stroud's cellblock, a guard informed him that Prisoner Number 8154 had been drawing geometry symbols on his cell wall, copying them from his cellmate's book. The guard said defacing walls was a violation and asked permission to throw Stroud into a punishment cell known as the hole. But the warden was fascinated. He reviewed Stroud's prison record and found it was fairly good, with the exception of the knifing at McNeil. The warden reprimanded Stroud for writing on the walls, but authorized him to receive drawing instruments. These were brought to his cell by a dumbfounded guard.

Safecracker Eddie was taking a correspondence course in higher mathematics. Stroud read some of the math problems while Eddie slept and found he could solve them far faster than the more educated safecracker. Stroud enrolled himself and finished the ten-month course in four months. He then dazzled his Kansas State College instructors by breezing through courses in astronomy and structural engineering with straight A grades. Both courses were prison favorites, astronomy because it gave the prisoners a feeling of spaciousness and structural engineering because it enabled them to think about ways to escape. Stroud discovered the Leavenworth library and became a serious student, tearing through books and scientific magazines at a ferocious rate. He sucked up knowledge like a sponge. One of his teachers reported Stroud received a high grade in a course called Strength of Materials, which required knowledge of geometry, trigonometry, and differential calculus.

When *Scientific American* magazine held a contest that included a problem in astronomy, Stroud wrote a pages-long answer with multiple equations and won an honorable mention. His avid reading brought him ultimately to theosophy, a religion based on Buddhism and metaphysics. "Enthralled by his reading," author Gaddis wrote, "Stroud embraced the brotherhood of Karma, thought-transference and reincarnation." Stroud felt he could send his spirit beyond the walls around him. He joined the Kansas City Theosophical Society, a group whose members visited him and later provided funding for his legal efforts.

Stroud's soaring intellect was still grounded by the reality of the prison bars around him. His hatreds grew and he became a maker of knives, kept carefully hidden and sold or bartered to his fellow inmates. Long hours of study and poor prison food affected his health; in early 1915 he was diagnosed with kidney disease. He lost weight and his attitude grew worse.

In 1915 the war in Europe caused further worsening of Leavenworth's food and a reduction in guard numbers. Passage of the Harrison Special Tax Act resulted in imprisonment of thousands of drug users, and narcotics flowed into the prison. One enterprising group of inmates organized a counterfeiting ring, producing phony bills for use both inside and outside Leavenworth's walls. A crackdown came and additional guards were assigned.

One new guard, Andrew F. Turner, came from Atlanta, where the rumor mill reported inmates there marked him for attack. They said he clubbed an elderly prisoner, fracturing his skull. A month after Turner's arrival, Stroud was sent to the prison hospital for treatment of his weakened kidneys. He remained there for twenty-six days, and the combination of his intellect and poor health drew the attention of the head nurse, who was also a prisoner. The nurse asked the doctor to return Stroud to his cell with orders to avoid work. The special attention grated on guard Turner, who decided Stroud was a discipline problem.

Stroud's mother had moved to Juneau before his trial and lived there for years afterward with her youngest son, Marc. She prospered as the owner of a rooming house. In early 1916, when Stroud was twenty-six, he received word that his eighteen-year-old brother would be visiting him in the spring. Marc arrived on a Saturday in March but was denied access due to a Leavenworth policy against Saturday visits. In his cell, Stroud found a note attached to a basket of fruit and candy. The note said Marc had arrived from Juneau and would try again to see him. Stroud was furious; Saturday visits were sometimes allowed and his brother's treatment seemed outrageous.

That night Turner caught Stroud whispering to a fellow inmate about his brother being turned away. Silence was the rule and whispering was a violation. If Turner reported it, Stroud would lose his visitor privileges. The guard was determined to report the violation and passed word he would do so. The next day Stroud approached Turner in the huge dining hall, where all eleven hundred prisoners were at lunch. The two exchanged words and Turner raised his club. The guard tried to strike but Stroud grabbed the club with both hands, then freed his left hand and drove a knife into Turner's chest. Turner fell dead on the floor. Nearby prisoners began to rise from their tables, but other guards rushed toward them. The prisoners sat down meekly; Stroud dropped the knife and was taken to solitary confinement.

Marc was shattered, certain his visit had caused the clash that resulted in the guard's death and new murder charges against his brother. Marc cabled his mother, insisting that she stay in Juneau. But Elizabeth sold her rooming house, took the first available boat to Seattle, then a train to Kansas City. There she hired a prominent attorney to defend her son.

Stroud was unrepentant about the killing. Gaddis writes that Stroud told a fellow prisoner that "the guard took sick of heart trouble. I guess you could call it a heart puncture. I never have given them any reason for my doing it, so they won't have much to work on; only that I killed him, and that won't do much good. I admit that much."

On May 27 a federal judge found Stroud guilty of first-degree murder and sentenced him to be hanged on

July 21. His lawyer appealed, and the trial was nullified on grounds that the judge had bypassed the law requiring a jury to decide whether a defendant should receive the death penalty.

Stroud saw his attack on Turner as a blow against the prison system, a blow of which he was rather proud. Prison officials still wanted to hang him, so they improved his food to make certain he didn't die before he could be killed. The better diet improved his health. The death penalty had been outlawed in Kansas, but state law did not apply within the federal prison. Stroud was retried and found guilty, but the jury recommended against hanging. He was sentenced instead to life imprisonment

Stroud's lawyers were happy with the verdict, but Stroud felt he should have been acquitted altogether and freed from prison. Prosecutors wanted another chance at him, hoping to send him to the gallows, so they readily agreed to a reversal on the basis of errors in the trial. The prisoner had been in solitary for more than two years when he was brought out for a third trial. The former prison nurse, who had been released and pardoned, testified in Stroud's defense. The nurse was now an ordained minister and successful businessman. Stroud was found guilty and sentenced to die, but the sentence caused a public uproar that unnerved prison officials. The Leavenworth warden vowed that if Stroud were not hung, this murderer of a guard would spend his life in solitary.

The defense lawyers appealed to the U.S. Supreme Court. While waiting, Stroud was allowed frequent visitors; he also wrote and studied music. A visitor brought him an old violin, which he learned to play while composing his own tunes, though Stroud's screeching music was unpopular with the other prisoners in solitary.

In 1920 the Supreme Court upheld Stroud's death sentence, and prison officials built a gallows in the exercise yard outside his cell window. Stroud's mother appealed to President Woodrow Wilson and later to first lady Edith Bolling Wilson. The governor of Kansas and members of the Kansas Legislature signed Elizabeth Stroud's petition. She also brought letters of support from Marshal Herbert Faulkner, the man to whom Stroud had surrendered in Juneau, and from Territorial Judge T. J. Lyons, his first lawyer. Elizabeth Stroud went to Washington and made repeated visits to the White House. Finally the first lady took Mrs. Stroud's papers to the president. She returned with the ailing Woodrow Wilson's scrawl across the execution order, "Commuted to life. W. W." Both felt Stroud's original sentence for killing Dahmer was excessive given the low character of the victim and Dahmer's attack on Kitty O'Brien.

Within hours the warden visited Stroud to inform him that his sentence was commuted and that all his privileges were thereby revoked. The warden told the press that Stroud would remain in solitary confinement for the rest of his life. When Stroud's mother protested, the warden claimed that Stroud was isolated for his own protection. Stroud asked his mother to stop her protests, saying he preferred solitary, where he was free to study and improve his mind.

Stroud was determined to help his mother, who had virtually bankrupted herself in his defense. He took up painting and turned out many small seasonal cards, sending them to his mother for sale to her friends.

One hot and windy June day in 1920, Stroud found three tiny sparrows in a nest that had blown into the exercise yard from a tree outside the wall. The mother bird hovered nearby but was unable to help her young. Stroud carried the nest to his cell, placed a sock over a light bulb to heat it, and wrapped the warm sock around the tiny birds. When his evening meal arrived, he fed them bread soaked in vegetable soup. The sparrows were ravenous. When his bread ran out, he fed them pieces of cockroaches and beetles he found in corners of his cell.

The next day, two of the birds were hopping about but one limped badly on a broken leg. Stroud fashioned a splint with a wooden match and a thread, then requested that the prison library send him every book it had on birds. In September, Stroud asked to see the deputy warden, a Mr. Fletcher, who loved birds. When Fletcher arrived he found the sparrows were thriving and Stroud had taught them tricks, responding to his whistle and finger snaps to perch and fly where he directed.

The deputy warden was enchanted. Stroud snapped twice and two of the sparrows flew to his bed, lying with their feet in the air. Fletcher laughed heartily and asked: "How in hell did you get them to play dead?" Stroud said it had just taken time and patience. Fletcher authorized an order for birdseed.

When prison restrictions loosened enough to allow prisoners to keep canaries as pets, Stroud decided he could raise the birds and sell them to help his mother. He ordered canaries and improvised feeding and watering devices from pop bottles and a cage from wooden soapboxes, all bought from guards and fellow inmates with cigarettes. Stroud began an intensive study of canaries and wrote about his findings. The birds were carried from the prison and sold by his mother, fifty-three of them in 1925 alone. His cell was crammed with birdcages.

At his request, Elizabeth Stroud subscribed to the *Roller Canary Journal* and brought the magazines to him at Leavenworth. He read every word. Stroud's cell became a regular stopping point for community visitors. The warden was proud to show the man and his flock, which grew as Stroud built more cages. Stroud read books on biology, chemistry, physiology, and zoology. Whenever one of his birds died, he dissected it with a razor blade and studied its internal organs. He began writing letters to *Roller Canary Journal* with questions and comments about his birds, which were often published. Stroud developed a following as an expert on canaries—though beyond that, most readers knew him only as a man with an address in Kansas City.

When his canaries became sick, he studied their problems and experimented on them. From his findings he wrote authoritative magazine articles and answered letters from worried bird owners. Stroud was convinced he could serve society better as a free man with access to libraries and laboratories, and he used his success with birds as the basis for frequent appeals for freedom. All were denied.

Stroud's success as a bird breeder encouraged prison officials to allow other prisoners to develop handicrafts and related small businesses. Since the convicts were for the most part a bunch of crooks, the inevitable happened and some small enterprises blossomed into rackets. Stroud was allowed to expand his bird laboratory into an adjoining and empty cell, but prison officials grew furious when they found him using laboratory equipment to make whiskey. In 1931 a crackdown came and restrictions were ordered on prison businesses. Stroud was ordered to close down and get rid of the birds. That ended his career as an active birder, but not his fame.

He wrote two well-regarded books, *Stroud's Digest on the Diseases of Birds* and *Diseases of Canaries.* In 1942 he was transferred from Leavenworth to the maximum security prison on Alcatraz Island, off California, becoming one of its best-known prisoners, his fame an irritant to his captors.

Stroud's story became known to author Gaddis, who then wrote *Birdman of Alcatraz,* which was published in 1955 and became a best seller. The book brought enormous national attention to Stroud's case, resulting in an upwelling of support for his cause and further irritating prison officials. The book was made into the movie starring Burt Lancaster, winning Lancaster an Academy Award. The warden refused to allow the movie to be shown at Alcatraz.

When Stroud's health declined in the late 1950s, he was transferred to the medical center for federal prisoners in Springfield, Missouri. He was found dead there on November 21, 1963, by friend and convicted spy Morton Sobell, after fifty-four years behind bars.

chapter five

THE MURDEROUS CHERUB

Tom Faccio couldn't believe such a young girl would be carrying a real gun, which looked like a cowboy pistol, so he tried to take it away. That's when an intended robbery turned into a killing spree.

Tom Faccio was eating dinner when a young girl knocked on his kitchen door and asked for help. Faccio's wife Ann and her sister, Emilia Elliott, were watching the evening news. They were elderly and cautious people, the kind who peer out to see who is at the door before opening it. They lived in a quiet Anchorage neighborhood relatively free of crime, but you could never be too careful.

When Faccio looked out, he saw the pudgy but rather cherubic face of a fourteen-year-old girl peering hopefully back at him, a plea on her lips. Faccio was a kindly man who would help a person in trouble if he could. He opened the door, the girl pointed a pistol at him, and the nightmare began.

The bodies of the Faccios and Emilia Elliott were found next morning by the Faccios' son, Tom, who became concerned when he tried to call his mother and got no answer. Young Tom walked to the house from his own nearby cabin and found all three had been shot and killed. His father and aunt had been bound with neckties and his mother lay dead in an upstairs bedroom. Young Tom flew into a grief-stricken rage, kicking out a glass storm door before calling his girlfriend, then police. Neighbors reported hearing his anguished screams piercing the quiet.

The elder Tom Faccio had once been a coal miner in Wyoming, where he was born into a large Italian family during the Great Depression. Grinding poverty forced his parents to send him to live with a Mexican family, where he was put to work in the coal mines of Rock Springs, Wyoming. Tom learned to speak Italian and Spanish, as well as English, and throughout his life he peppered his conversation with expressions from all three languages.

Faccio worked hard and made astute investments. He was a construction worker with the instincts of a businessman. He came to Anchorage from California in 1949 to build military housing for Elmendorf Air Force Base. A few years later he opened a plumbing supply store on Mountain View Drive. Faccio was a down-home kind of man, a gregarious and friendly sort who made customers feel at home in Tom's Plumbing and Heating. He would go out of his way to make sure each person found the part they needed and went away a satisfied customer.

When he died at age sixty-nine, Faccio was believed to be a wealthy man—owner of several Alaska businesses, land in Anchorage, Kenai, and Arizona, and oil wells in Kentucky. Ann Faccio was seventy and Emilia Elliott was seventy-six when death came to their door in the early evening of April 22, 1985. Emilia had retired as a nurse ten years before and moved in with the Faccios to keep Ann company during Tom's frequent business trips.

The Faccios had three grown children: Sharon Nahorney, an interior decorator and wife of an Anchorage orthodontist; Janice Lienhart, whose husband managed Tom's plumbing supply store; and young Tom, who had been born to a relative and was adopted by the Faccios.

In the 1950s, Tom Faccio built a large home in East Anchorage on two acres bordering Russian Jack Springs Park. The three-level house sat on a hill in a spot noted for its solitude and spectacular scenery. "It was the peacefulness and the view—that's why Daddy built it there," Nahorney later told a newspaper reporter. "We could look out the window and see Mount McKinley and the Inlet, and outside all we could hear were the birds." Both of the Faccio daughters were married in the house. Parts of the surrounding neighborhood deteriorated through the years, but the Faccio property was large enough to be relatively unaffected by the decline.

The exterior of the Faccio home was relatively plain, but Tom had used part of his accumulating wealth to make the inside quite luxurious. The house sported one of the first imported Italian crystal chandeliers ever seen in Alaska. The house had a cascading waterfall, a sweeping grand staircase, a fully equipped gymnasium, a large barbecue pit, and a "weather room" where a person could get a suntan or watch an indoor rainfall. The house had a burglar alarm, which was never used when the family was at home. Ann was afraid she would accidentally set it off when she opened a window.

Much of Ann Faccio's life revolved around her husband, her children, and her grandchildren, on whom she lavished gifts and attention. Emilia Elliott was a stay-at-home person who enjoyed puttering in her garden and making bread in the Faccio kitchen. She kept a journal for many years, each day recording the sunlight and temperature data, dutifully jotting them down each evening as the Channel 2 weather forecaster read that day's statistics over the air.

Winona Fletcher came from a family that had been dysfunctional for several generations. As a girl, Winona's grandmother had been sexually molested by a family member. When she complained, she was sent to a home for wayward girls. She pleaded to be allowed to stay with the family, but was told by her mother (Winona's great-grandmother) that she was a bad little girl and that nobody would ever love her. She was raised without compassion, and she raised her own children the same way.

Winona's mother left home at age fifteen and married shortly afterward, giving birth before her sixteenth birthday to Winona. An alcoholic, the mother gave Winona her first drink at age six. The child tried marijuana about a year later. By age twelve, Winona sometimes drank six or seven beers at a time and was working as a prostitute. By fourteen she drank a third of a fifth of rum every day. She used LSD, cocaine, Valium, and amphetamines.

Winona's mother moved from Oregon to Alaska in 1983 to be near her boyfriend, an ex-convict who had been booted out of the military for drug use and served time in a California prison. They stayed for a time at Clare House, an Anchorage home for women and children in need. The home's director later remembered

Winona as an angry and troubled little girl with a foul mouth and a swaggering manner. She wore black leather pants and studs and, despite the swagger, had persistent feelings of worthlessness.

Winona began running away from home at an early age and was somewhat older than her classmates at Clark Junior High School in Anchorage because she had been held back through the years by a learning disability. She was a sporadic student who missed more than half her classes, but teachers said she would disappear for days at a time, then show up and ask for the assignments she had missed. She would complete them all, and she tried hard to please her teachers. An *Anchorage Daily News* article quoted one as saying: "She just seemed to be one of those kids that needed a hug more than others. She had the demeanor of a tough little cookie, but this kid was like a sponge for adult approval."

Despite her anger and tough exterior, Winona was a religious young woman. She owned and frequently read a Bible, sometimes quoting from it to her friends. In February 1985, Winona moved in with Cordel Boyd, a nineteen-year-old black man and West Anchorage High School dropout who raised money to buy drugs by bur-glarizing houses. Her only criminal record up to that point was an arrest for shoplifting. She gloried in Boyd's attentions.

The two began burglarizing homes together, though they sometimes seemed to work alone. On March 21 Boyd was caught while breaking into a home on West Thirteenth Avenue. He was released the following day on one thousand dollars bail. Four days later, on the same day charges were brought against him for the March 21 job, Boyd burglarized a home on S Street. The burglary loot was acquired primarily to raise cash to buy drugs. Occasionally Boyd and Winona found weapons, includ-ing pistols, and they kept a few of those for their personal use. After all, burglary could sometimes be a high-risk profession.

On April 2 the young couple hit yet another home, on Laurel Street. Eight days later the charges against Boyd were amended to add this burglary. He failed to show up at a court hearing April 18 and a warrant was issued for his arrest.

Boyd and Winona lived in an abandoned apartment a few blocks from the Faccio home. One morning they walked by and noticed that the Faccio place was secluded and expensive, a rich family's home. They walked away, but the attractions of the Faccio home stuck in their minds. Until now their crimes had been primarily breaking and entering into unoccupied houses. But the possibility of robbery in a fancy house with old and affluent residents offered the possibility of both cash from wallets and purses as well as expensive merchandise.

On their way to the Faccio house on April 22, Boyd and Winona talked about what to do with anyone inside. Boyd said he didn't want to kill anybody and would wear a ski mask. But fourteen-year-old Winona and her youthful face were their ticket to entering the house. She could not be masked, and she argued that something would have to be done about the old people.

Monday mornings were always busy at Tom's Plumbing, and Tom Faccio was at the customer counter as usual. Contractors came and went, picking up supplies for their week's work. At one point, Tom paused to take a telephone call. An oil investment had paid off and he was due for some extra cash. He called home with the news and was surprised when Ann began crying. "Why are you crying?" he asked. Ann said she was just so happy because there were so many things she wanted to buy for her grandchildren.

About 1:00 p.m., Janice Lienhart picked up her mother and took her to Muldoon Community Assembly, where Janice's fifteen-year-old daughter Tamara was singing in a choir competition. Janice's Aunt Emilia stayed at home and puttered in her garden behind the Faccio home.

Janice dropped her mother off at the house about five and said good-bye. Shortly afterward, the Faccios' adopted son, Tom, dropped by. Ann gave him some chicken and shooed him away before her husband arrived. The elder Tom Faccio and his son did not get along and Ann wanted to have the rest of her husband's dinner ready when he got home.

Before leaving the store, Tom's bookkeeper, Marcie Clark, made reservations for him on the next day's commuter flight to Soldotna. Tom was planning to spend a few days resting up there on his new boat, a cruiser he had christened *Tomcatt*. Marcie and her boss engaged in their customary good-natured banter before she left. He told her she should go down to the boat and he would stay and work. She said, "No, you go and I'll stay."

Tom drove home, sat down at his dining room table, and dug into a meal of salad, soup, and the remaining chicken. Ann and Emilia watched the evening news. Ann was an avid news watcher and Emilia was, as always, poised to jot down the sunlight and temperature data read off by the Channel 2 forecaster. All three looked up when they heard a knock on the kitchen door. Tom put down his coffee and went to answer. He peered out the window to see a young woman standing on his porch and then opened the door with his customary caution.

When Tom opened the door, Winona Fletcher pointed a .22 caliber revolver at him. Faccio didn't believe such a young girl would be carrying a real gun, which looked like a cowboy pistol, so he grabbed it and tried to take it away. The gun went off. Nobody was hit, but the shot brought Ann Faccio running to the kitchen. Just then Cordel Boyd stepped into the kitchen waving his own pistol, a ski mask covering his face.

The two youngsters herded Tom and Ann into the dining room. Boyd watched them while Winona searched the house. She found Emilia hiding on a patio and ordered her at gunpoint to join Tom and Ann in the dining room. Boyd gave Winona his pistol and Winona pointed both guns at her elderly hostages while he searched the house for something to tie them up with.

Boyd grabbed a fistful of Tom's neckties and bound their wrists. At that point Ann began showing signs of physical distress, which made the young intruders think she was having a heart attack. Winona gave Boyd back his pistol, then ordered Ann upstairs and into a bedroom. There Ann fell to her knees and began praying for Winona and begging for her own life to be spared. Winona raised her pistol and pulled the trigger. The shot missed, hitting a wall, and Winona laughed. She then placed the gun three inches from the head of the still-praying Ann. "Shut up, bitch," she growled and fired again.

Tom Faccio heard the shot and called out to his wife, asking what had happened. Boyd told him his wife had just been shot. Tom began crying.

Winona returned to the downstairs room and walked over to Emilia Elliott, who was lying on the floor on her back, hands tied with a necktie, her head resting on a pillow that Boyd had placed there. Winona shot Emilia in the head.

Tom Faccio had worked his hands free but was now in complete shock. He begged them not to kill him and offered the couple cash from his pockets. Boyd took seven hundred dollars, then Winona shot Tom in the chest, wounding him. Boyd swapped guns with Winona—he was afraid his large-caliber weapon would make too much noise. Tom was spitting up blood and Boyd felt the man was suffering. He finished him off with a bullet in the head, then the two young intruders ran from the house.

The killers left few clues. Winona had unknowingly left behind several fingerprints, but the prints matched nothing in police files. Anchorage police detectives and crime scene experts spent more than a week at the scene, collecting and bagging evidence and reenacting the crime based on what they could find. Among other things, investigators determined that the entire robbery probably had taken about forty-five minutes. Tom Faccio still had two thousand dollars in cash in his pockets. Also left behind were several of Tom's firearms, valuable jewelry, and other expensive and easy to carry items.

Meanwhile even civilians got involved in the investigation, with volunteers using metal detectors to sweep the high grass and trees in the neighborhood, hoping to find a murder weapon. Since the Faccios' adopted son, Tom, was the first person on the scene—and since young Tom did not get along with his father—he became an early suspect both in the eyes of the police and his own family. Young Tom had a reputation as a brawler. He had a record for drunken driving and malicious destruction of property, and was on probation for assault in a bar fight. He took two lie-detector tests, passing both, and was quickly eliminated as a suspect. "God," he told his sister Janice, "can you imagine how I felt walking into that house and seeing my parents dead? It tore me apart, and now everyone thinks I did it."

The initial investigation turned up numerous clues, but none of them pointed to a real suspect. The Crimestoppers citizens group posted a ten thousand dollar reward for information leading to arrests, an amount which the two Faccio daughters quickly raised to fifty thousand.

Two weeks after the shooting, a guilt-racked street person told investigators that he was one of a group of killers responsible for the Faccio murders. He told police a believable story and led them to the Faccio house. Police worked round-the-clock for four days, checking his story.

"But there were things he didn't know, either," an investigator said. "He finally broke down and told us he was lying. Know what? Everything he knew he'd gotten by watching television at the Brother Francis Shelter," a facility for the homeless in downtown Anchorage.

The large reward brought a flood of calls and tips, all of which led nowhere. Six weeks after the killings, the eleven investigators still working the case began to worry that the triple murder might never be solved. They had found five hundred fingerprints in the house, but almost all had been identified and led to nothing. One detective lamented that it would have been helpful if the killers had trashed the house or written on the walls.

On May 30, Winona and Boyd broke into an apartment on West Twenty-Seventh Avenue. Police found them there and Winona was arrested, but Boyd got away. At police headquarters, she admitted to participating in burglaries with Boyd back to February. While she was being questioned, Boyd called police headquarters to find out what was happening to her.

The call was traced to a pay phone at the Sears Mall and police squad cars raced there from throughout the city. Boyd saw them moving into position around the mall and fled. He hid in various parts of the store complex, climbed to the roof and ran across it, then jumped into a metal trash bin. After an hour, he ran across Northern Lights Boulevard toward Fireweed Lane. Police caught up to him outside the Fireweed Theater, arrested him, and brought him to headquarters.

Once under arrest, Boyd tried to make a deal, offering information about cocaine dealers in exchange for leniency on the burglary charges. He told his interrogator that, in any case, he would "beat this rap" and be out on the street on bail within a couple of days. His bail was raised to eighty thousand dollars.

But Boyd was an ignorant braggart who admitted to a cellmate that he and his girlfriend had killed the Faccios and Emilia Elliott. After he was released, the cellmate got a call from Boyd asking him to lean on Winona and get her to recant her confession on the burglaries. During the conversation, Boyd talked in detail about the murders. The cellmate, having heard about the fifty thousand dollar reward, recorded the conversation. He then called Crimestoppers, said he wanted to claim the money, and told about the tape. When investigators listened to the tape, they obtained a court order allowing them to record all conversations between Boyd and Winona for the next seven days.

Boyd was becoming increasingly worried that Winona might confess to the murders as well as the burglaries—and name him. He called the ex-cellmate numerous times from jail, talking about the killings and urging the cellmate to help get Winona out of the juvenile detention center. In the meantime, investigators

checked Winona's fingerprints against those found at
the Faccio house; they matched. Both Boyd and Winona
were charged with first-degree murder.

When their arrests hit the news, a man turned a
.22 revolver over to police, saying he had bought it
from Cordel Boyd in a bar in late April, paying ten
dollars for it. Investigators determined it was the
murder weapon and had been stolen by Boyd during
one of his earlier burglaries. Both Winona and Boyd
pleaded guilty in adult court and each was sentenced
to 297 years in jail.

Winona's initial hearings were in Juvenile Court
because of her age. Though Winona was later remanded
to adult court, the Faccio daughters found themselves
barred from the initial hearings because the defendant was a juvenile. They were shocked once again.
They had gone so long before knowing who killed their
parents. Then when the truth came out, the court system seemed more intent on protecting the young killer
than it was in providing justice for the victims' families.

The daughters were frustrated by being left out of
the legal system and found the situation only marginally
better during the adult court hearings. Though still grief-
stricken, Sharon and Janice channeled their emotions
and their energy into forming a nonprofit organization,
Victims for Justice, which through the years has coun-
seled hundreds of victims' families and won important
changes in the Alaska legal system.

For years they wrote letters to newspaper editors
and buttonholed politicians. Among the changes the
daughters wrought: where previously a person had to
be physically injured to be considered a victim, the

definition was expanded to include those close enough to the victim to be emotionally devastated. Victims may now have their say at sentencing hearings in otherwise private criminal juvenile trials; police may now fingerprint juvenile defendants just as they do adults; and when juveniles commit violent crimes, the doors of their court proceedings are now open to their victims.

A judge later amended Winona's sentence to 135 years, making her eligible for parole in 2031, at age sixty, and whether she is eventually freed will depend on how she behaves behind bars. So far Winona has had two children while in prison, despite the fact that having sex is not allowed for prisoners and is considered quite difficult to manage. The babies were taken from Winona and given to her mother to be raised—a puzzling decision given that trial testimony and news accounts at the time of the killings suggested that Winona's mother was herself a troubled woman and that Winona's own upbringing was a factor in her aberrant behavior.

At one point Winona was sent to a North Dakota prison that offered a special program for youthful offenders. In 1993 she was kicked out of that facility for having sex with an inmate and was returned to Alaska to serve out the balance of her sentence.

chapter six

THE NEWMAN FAMILY MASSACRE

Anchorage police were determined to catch the murderer. They assembled a task force of a dozen detectives and patrol officers. It was one of the most intensive murder investigations in Alaska history.

Nancy Newman was a thirty-two-year-old waitress with two beautiful daughters—Melissa, eight, and Angela, three, both blue-eyed strawberry blondes. Nancy was short, blonde, and slender, a quiet woman who socialized little with her co-workers at Gwennie's Old Alaska Restaurant. The notable exception was her sister, Cheryl Chapman, also a waitress at the popular restaurant in Anchorage's Spenard neighborhood.

Nancy was a very reliable employee who rarely took time off, so the Gwennie's staff worried when she didn't show up on Saturday, March 14, 1987. Her phone went unanswered, so on Sunday—with still no sign of Nancy—a worried staffer called Nancy's sister. Cheryl drove with her husband, Paul, to Nancy's apartment on Eide Street. Cheryl stood worried and trembling at the door, keys fumbling in her hand, and rang the doorbell. Getting no answer and trembling too much to manage the lock, she gave the keys to her husband, who slowly opened the door.

Through the partially opened doorway they could see Melissa's stilled feet. They pushed open the door further and walked into one of the most horrific murder scenes ever reported in Anchorage. Cheryl stood in shock while Paul walked through the apartment. He came back to tell her that everyone was dead. The sound of Cheryl's anguished screaming can be heard in the tape of Paul's call to police.

Three-year-old Angie was on the floor of her bedroom, her throat slashed from ear to ear, nearly decapitated. She had a gash on one hand, apparently received while trying to protect herself. The child was covered with blood except for a cleaned swath extending from her chest to her crotch, apparently wiped with a washcloth.

Melissa lay on the floor of her room. Her nightgown was pulled up to her chest and a pair of panties lay a few feet away. A pillowcase was knotted around her neck, strangling her; another was tied around one wrist. Both her legs were bent at the knee and splayed open, her crotch covered with blood. She had been raped with a blunt object.

In the master bedroom, Nancy lay strangled on her bed, a blue pillowcase knotted around her neck. Her face was bruised and she had been struck several times with a blunt instrument. Her nightshirt was pulled up around her neck, her breasts and vagina exposed. The scene devastated Cheryl and her husband and sickened even the experienced police investigators who pored over the apartment for weeks afterward.

Cheryl called Nancy's husband, John, who was in California finishing up a three-month training program. John was a former airline equipment operator who had been injured in a forklift rollover at Prudhoe Bay and was being retrained to do locksmith and security work. He and Nancy had been married right after their high school graduation in Twin Falls, Idaho. They were a happy couple and hugely proud of their daughters.

At the end of their last shift together on Friday, Nancy and Cheryl had stayed for a drink to celebrate John's pending return from California. Nancy was planning to take a week off for their reunion. Another waitress said Nancy was "just so excited about Johnny coming home." John Newman returned to Anchorage stunned and unbelieving. He made the funeral arrangements in a daze. His family would be buried in Twin Falls in an oversize casket, allowing Nancy to rest through eternity with one of her daughters under each arm.

Anchorage police were determined to catch the murderer. They assembled a task force of a dozen detectives and patrol officers to work full-time on the case. It was one of the most intensive murder investigations in Alaska history. The team spent two weeks taking samples of blood, hair, fluids, clothing, fingerprints and footprints, carpet, and every other material they could find in the apartment. Among the evidence collected was a washcloth apparently used by the murderer to clean himself, and containing blood and feces. They vacuumed the floor and carefully bagged the dust and fibers drawn up by the machine. Every surface was checked for fingerprints. Hundreds of photographs and measurements were taken and the entire scene videotaped, bodies still in place. Officers roved the neighborhood asking residents if they had noticed any suspicious activities over the weekend, any strangers who didn't seem to belong there. "Did you see anything?" they asked. "Hear anything?"

Many of the samples were sent to the FBI laboratory at Quantico, Virginia, and Anchorage police conferred with the FBI's behavioral science experts. Computer checks were run to match aspects of the case with information on other crimes, criminals, and victims. The experts drew a personality profile of the person who might commit such a crime. The FBI lab reported that pubic hairs on the bloody washcloth carried lice egg casings matching lice residue found on the bodies of Melissa and Angie. The washcloth also contained green fibers from a pair of gloves found near Nancy's body, gloves that had been used to pull hair from Nancy's head. Missing from the apartment were the contents of a metal cookie jar where Nancy kept up to two hundred dollars in tips; also gone were Nancy's purse, checkbook, wallet, keys, jewelry, and a camera.

Autopsies were done on the three bodies at the new Alaska state crime lab. Dr. Michael Propst, a forensic pathologist, performed postmortem surgeries and developed evidence that would prove crucial at the trial. Using a laser, Propst found four hairs that belonged to none of the victims, as well as body fluids left by the killer. Three of the hairs were found on the bodies of Nancy and her daughters, the fourth was found on the washcloth.

The investigation was thorough and professional, a result of the Anchorage Police Department's having become one of the best in the nation. Where it had

once bobbled the investigation of serial killer Robert
Hansen, almost certainly enabling him to kill more
women, it was now organized into a highly effective
team. At its core was the Homicide Response Team,
organized three years before by Sergeant Mike Grimes,
one of the best police investigators ever to work in
Alaska. The team included five officers, several technical specialists, a lawyer, a videotape team, and a
still photographer.

Local lawyers said Grimes' homicide team con-
sistently went several steps farther than comparable
groups in other departments. One of the lawyers who
spoke admiringly of the homicide investigators was
Brant McGee, a defense attorney who occasionally
found himself trying to counter the evidence Grimes'
group dug up. While many police investigations fo-
cus primarily on getting enough evidence to arrest a
suspect, Grimes and his team kept digging until they had
enough for prosecutors to win their cases.

An FBI agent at the agency's behavioral science
unit looked at the mounting evidence and said the
murders were probably committed by someone who
had been in the Newman home before, someone who
felt comfortable being in the neighborhood early in
the morning, someone neighbors wouldn't even notice because he had a reason to be there. He said the
killer was likely someone who could keep himself
under control when things were going well, but fantasized rapes and killings and had probably assaulted
young girls before. It would not be unusual for such a
person to commit a sex murder and seem normal an
hour later.

Suspicion centered from the very beginning on John's nephew, Kirby Anthoney, twenty-three, who had lived with the Newman family briefly in 1985. Anthoney and his girlfriend came to Alaska after he abruptly left Twin Falls, where he was a prime suspect in the rape and near-fatal beating of a twelve-year-old girl left for dead in a campground. Idaho police did not pursue charges in the Twin Falls case because they couldn't prove Anthoney beat the girl; she was brain-damaged in the attack and couldn't identify him.

Anthoney denied involvement, though he had earlier confessed to a 1982 armed robbery in which he sprayed an elderly wheelchair-bound woman with Mace. He said he sprayed the disabling liquid on the woman to keep her from screaming. He later withdrew the confession and the case was dismissed. Despite his earlier statement about using the Mace, he was never convicted of the assault. He had also been arrested three times for burglary, three times for larceny, and once for disorderly conduct. Most of the charges were dismissed and he served no jail time.

Anthoney and his girlfriend stayed with the Newmans for about a month before heading off for jobs on a Dutch Harbor fishing boat. But two months later, Anthoney returned to Anchorage; he had been fired by the boat's skipper and kicked out by his girlfriend, who grew tired of his frequent beatings. The girlfriend had complained to the ship's production manager and asked that Anthoney be kept away from her, resulting in his being thrown off the ship.

In Anchorage, Anthoney asked Nancy if he could stay with the Newmans again and she agreed, not wanting to turn away family. Afterward Anthoney's father and the father's wife visited him. Father and son got into a fistfight at the Newman home when the father made a belittling remark, the fight ending when John broke it up. Anthoney was in tears. "All I ever wanted was for you to love and respect me," he shouted at his dad, "and you never would."

Nancy heard from Anthoney's mother that he was talking of suicide. Nancy was afraid he would harm himself around her daughters and asked him to leave. He did, moving in with another acquaintance, but he was furious.

The morning the bodies were found, two police officers went to where Anthoney was staying and knocked on the door. They told him that Nancy and the girls were dead and that he was a suspect. Anthoney's roommate later testified that Anthoney called his mother in Twin Falls and told her: "Sit down, Mom. . . . Nancy and the girls are dead. Settle down, Mom. . . . They won't tell me what happened to them, if they were raped or not. . . . But, Mom, they think I did it."

When officers interviewed him, Anthoney denied having a key to Nancy's apartment—though police knew that he did—and he was caught lying about his whereabouts between 8:30 and 10:30 on Saturday morning, the time that investigators believed the murders took place. The apartment door had not been forced, meaning that either the door was unlocked or the intruder had a key.

Anthoney said he had spent the night before the murders drinking and using cocaine at a dice-playing party across the street from his own apartment. He stayed up all night and went home when his roommate, Dan Grant, was getting ready to go to work. Grant said Anthoney left about 8:30 a.m., and police learned he was not seen again until after the time the murders were believed to have taken place. Anthoney gave police clothing he claimed he was wearing that

Saturday morning. Most of it seemed fairly clean, but one of the shoes contained a small, bright red droplet that looked a lot like blood. The shoe and a stained shirt were forwarded to the FBI lab.

The public was terrified by the murders, not knowing whether the killer was still in Anchorage and might kill again. Though police were pretty sure that it was Anthoney, they needed more evidence before they could bring charges and take him off the street. They ignored the pressure and told the news media they had run down more than five hundred leads, but none pointed to a specific suspect. Tips poured into police headquarters, many of them forwarded by the Crimestoppers organization. One came on a postcard to Mayor Tony Knowles. The investigating team would discuss none of them publicly.

Police interviewed Anthoney's roommate, suggesting that he let them know if Anthoney did anything unusual. An order went out within the police department that no unknown details of the murders were to be released to the public; the investigators wanted that information kept between themselves and the murderer.

While the crime lab ran its tests at Quantico, the task force in Anchorage decided to run a few tests themselves, psychological tests. They decided to mess with the suspect's mind and see what happened. They tailed Anthoney through town, making sure he noticed that he was followed. Then they removed the tail, then put it back, keeping him guessing. Two investigators talked to him frequently, one playing a friendly good cop, the other an antagonistic bad cop. When they determined he was sometimes lying to them to make his story conform to evidence they were finding, the officers tried lying to him to see what he would say.

Five days after the murders, Anthoney stopped for drinks at Chilkoot Charlie's, a popular Anchorage tavern. There he struck up a conversation with a female lighting consultant. He told the woman about the murders and that he was a suspect. He told her: "The worst thing was that the mom had to watch" the murder of her daughters. The woman said Anthoney was writing weird poems on napkins and handing them around the bar.

On April 13, Anthoney called the friendly cop to check on the status of the investigation. The officer asked to meet with him next day, saying he wanted to discuss hair and fiber evidence just back from Quantico. The morning of the meeting, Anthoney left a message saying he needed to help a friend with a truck and wouldn't be able to keep his appointment. Two days later, Anthoney's roommate, Dan Grant, called police and said Anthoney had climbed into his blue Ford truck that morning and was headed for the Canadian border. Anthoney had asked him to cover his escape, "to play dumb," Grant said, "to say he was not at home, that I didn't know where he was at."

Anchorage police notified U.S. Customs and the Royal Canadian Mounted Police at the Tok border crossing. Anthoney attempted to cross near midnight, but he was arrested and charged with driving while his license was suspended. He was taken to the Fairbanks Correctional Center and held there until more serious charges could be filed in Anchorage.

Meanwhile, Quantico reported that the fingerprints on Nancy's cookie jar matched Anthoney's, as did the various fluids recovered from the bodies and the washcloth. The Anchorage team found Nancy's camera, camera bag, and accessories at Anthoney's apartment. Witnesses reported that Anthoney had been paying for meals with rolls of coins, rolls like those Nancy kept in her cookie jar. Tests at Quantico on Anthoney's shirt showed it was stained with feces from Nancy Newman's body. Tests on the leather coat and sneakers Anthoney wore that day showed signs of human blood.

Anthoney's arrest and the lurid details of the murders fanned public outrage. One woman wrote a letter to the *Anchorage Daily News* longing for the days when such criminals could be publicly stoned or hung. If such were possible, she said, she would be in the front row and throw the first rock. Many writers called for bringing back the death penalty in Alaska, and one offered to throw the switch on an electric chair—for free.

Anthoney was quickly brought to Anchorage and charged with three counts of murder, two counts of raping Nancy and Melissa, and one count of kidnapping, the charge based on the fact that Melissa's hands had been bound. Outrage about the case resulted in some unusual precautions, including searching the bags of reporters and photographers attending his arraignment and patting them down for weapons. By the time he showed up in public, the once lice-infected Anthoney appeared to be a pleasant blond man with neatly trimmed hair and beard, the improvements apparently suggested by his government-supplied lawyers. Anyone looking at the defense table would have difficulty guessing which were lawyers and which the defendant.

Anthoney was not popular in jail. A fellow prisoner who had been arrested for killing four people beat him up, resulting in wounds that required six stitches to close. Kiven Collins was a cocaine dealer who had only meant to kill three people. The fourth, a fifteen-year-old girl, just happened to get into the line of fire. He said of Anthoney, "If I ever get another chance, he won't need no trial. There's never no need to kill a woman and two little girls. I have a young daughter myself."

At the start of his trial the following April, the prosecutor charged—and Anthoney's defense attorneys agreed—that on the morning of the murders, Anthoney had left an all-night party and gone home in time to see his roommate leave for work, and that Anthoney then disappeared from 8:30 to 10:30 a.m., the time of the Newman family massacre.

The prosecutor told the jury that Anthoney sometimes wrote suggestive poetry. He read them this stanza:

> Subjecting to his wild assault
> Losing all the mind's reason
> Captured in an addictive vault
> Twisting life's dimensions

Anthoney attended the trial each day neatly dressed in a sports jacket, with a starched shirt and tie. When word reached his legal team that several spectators and one juror reported that his eyes seemed evil, Anthoney began wearing glasses with blue-tinted lenses.

The trial was especially difficult for Nancy's husband, John, who had moved back to Twin Falls to start over far from the crime scene. John was allowed to sit through the trial for the week before he testified. When called to the witness stand, he was just ten feet from Anthoney. When a lawyer asked him one question about his wife, John broke into convulsive sobs and had to leave the courtroom, but he returned and finished his testimony. Some spectators broke into tears as they heard John's tortured voice.

Janice Lienhart and Sharon Nahorney, whose parents and aunt were murdered just three years before, sat in the courtroom and tried to help John. They were the daughters of Tom and Ann Faccio and niece to Emilia Elliott, who were murdered by a fourteen-year-old girl and her partner during a 1985 robbery. They had been frustrated by the legal system during the girl's trial and came to the Kirby Anthoney trial to see if they could help.

John told Janice Lienhart that everyone in Twin Falls knew what had happened in Anchorage. One man approached him on the sidewalk and asked how he had managed not to kill himself yet. Janice encouraged John to talk about his feelings, to get the emotions out where he could deal with them. When John ran from the courtroom, she followed him to his hotel. There she found him hurling things at the wall of his room. She told him that her husband had gone to the firing range after her parents were killed and shooting seemed to help him. He wanted to try it, so Janice borrowed her husband's pistol and drove him to a range on the south side of town. He blazed away through the afternoon. "It really freaked out the police when I told them," she said later, "but it sure helped John."

The jury watched the videotape of the horrendous murder scene with the bodies, each in its own room, each splayed open with genitals exposed. Jurors could see blood spattered on the walls and furniture and on the bodies. The prosecutor told them that Nancy's sister had to use a key to enter the apartment that morning and that all doors had been locked after the murders. And Nancy's tip jar and valuables were taken without ransacking the house, suggesting that they were taken by someone who knew where to find them.

In the end the jury found Anthoney guilty on all counts. When Anthoney arrived in the courtroom, he turned to Nancy's husband and said: "You're a fool, John." Then shortly afterward he added: "I love you with all my heart."

John Newman blew up. "Don't you talk to me," he shouted, lunging for Anthoney as friends held him down. "Don't you even talk to me".

chapter seven

THE BANK ROBBER
NEXT DOOR

The killer's surrender nearly denied him a moment of national infamy. The TV series "America's Most Wanted" was about to broadcast his story. The show's producers decided to air the segment anyway.

Paul Stavenjord first came to public attention on August 4, 1971, when he and two friends robbed the Seward branch of the First National Bank of Anchorage. The heist was a scatterbrained scheme, one that had members of the pursuing police dragnet scratching their heads, wondering how stupid a robbery gang could be.

Stavenjord was then twenty years old. His buddies and fellow stickup artists were Robert G. Jett, twenty-two, and Randall M. Simmons, nineteen. On their big day, the gang took a young girl hostage on their way into the bank, then stormed in waving two pistols and a sawed-off shotgun. Stavenjord and Simmons ordered the eight bank employees and fourteen customers to lie on the floor, then cleaned out the teller drawers while Jett guarded the door. They argued with the bank manager, who reluctantly produced the vault key. Stavenjord held open a green rubberized bag while Simmons stuffed it with cash.

There is only one road in and out of Seward, a forty-mile spur running south through the Chugach Mountains from an intersection with the Seward Highway. If the robbers had tried to get away in their car, police based in Soldotna or traveling the highway could have driven to the intersection and set up a roadblock well before the Stavenjord gang could reach the spot.

But the three robbers had thought that problem through and come up with an alternate escape route complete with a fiery diversion. Their car was a 1964 Chevy Nova stolen in Anchorage the day before. They brought along a cache of dynamite, with which they planned to either blow up or booby-trap the car.

But the robbery had not gone unnoticed. The city's only on-duty police officer watched from outside, unwilling to enter and start a gunfight in the crowded lobby. When the robbers fled, a city employee followed them in his utility truck as they drove up Lowell Canyon Road at the base of Mount Marathon. The officer ran into the bank to check on the customers and employees.

The robbers planned to flee on foot through the mountains, make their way across the rugged Kenai Peninsula to the city of Kenai, and then disappear somewhere to enjoy their swag. Stavenjord planned to spend the coming winter hunting and trapping along the Yukon River.

Their preparations before the robbery had included setting up three camps on the Kenai side of the mountains. But the robbers headed up Mount Marathon with no real understanding of how rugged the country could be. Nor did they realize how heavy their loot would be. Stuffed with $150,000, the green rubber bag weighed more than forty pounds. When it proved too heavy, the gang stashed the cash in an alder thicket, where their pursuers found it.

When the trail through the mountains proved too tough, the robbers turned back to Seward, hoping to lose themselves in the crowd. Searching everywhere for them was a swarming posse of twenty-five FBI agents, State Troopers, and town police, augmented by local citizens deputized and armed for the hunt. The road out of town and the local airstrip were sealed off. A helicopter swept over the mountains.

The gang camped briefly below tree line on Mount Marathon and then split up. Three days after the robbery, Seward Police Chief Bill Bagron was parked beside a roadblock when Stavenjord popped out of the bushes about fifty feet from him. Stavenjord was carrying a loaded pistol and a dagger, but he failed to notice Bagron's police cruiser before stepping onto the highway. The chief took him into custody with no problem. Shortly afterward the other two gang members were found in a Seward restaurant, eating bowls of chili.

All three had previous police records for everything from receiving and concealing stolen property to armed robbery and larceny. They were indicted by a federal grand jury for armed bank robbery and received six-year prison terms. Stavenjord served his sentence at the federal penitentiary in Lompoc, California, and was released on probation in 1975.

Paul Stavenjord had a difficult childhood in Everett, Washington. His mother divorced his father, telling the children their dad was an alcoholic. She married twice more, but the boy's relationship with his stepfathers was rocky. The family moved to Seward in 1965. Shortly after his arrival, young Paul was expelled from ninth grade after calling African-Americans "coons" in front of a black teacher. He never went back to school.

Paul was a belligerent teenager given to dark moods, during which he would retreat to his bedroom and sit with a faraway look in his eyes, his head in his hands.

He was arrested five times in the next two years. His crimes included breaking into cabins, stealing a skiff and a car, and ransacking his girlfriend's house and returning with a gun, threatening to kill himself. He was serving time in an Anchorage juvenile facility in 1966 when his group took a field trip to play baseball at Central Junior High School. Stavenjord ran from the ball field, stole a car, and led police on a chase through city streets doing seventy miles an hour before being caught. He spent two more years at McLaughlin Youth Center and was released in 1968. Six months later, he robbed a liquor store in downtown Anchorage at gunpoint. The haul was $190. He was arrested and spent three more years behind bars. He told authorities he robbed to support a heroin addiction and had been using LSD for two years.

Stavenjord became a different man after serving time for the Seward bank heist. In effect, he went straight. He took a job with the Alaska Railroad, repairing and inspecting tracks. The work was difficult, requiring him to lift hundred-pound rails, but he had a long career with the line, staying for more than twenty years.

He fell in love, first with Chulitna—a wilderness area near the railroad, forty miles north of Talkeetna—then with Peggy Hogarty, a twenty-three-year-old waitress working in railcars. They were married and two years later, he and Peggy had a daughter, Rebecca. The family moved to Chulitna and built a cabin. They lived there for eleven years, making do with Paul's railroad salary and home-schooling Rebecca. Stavenjord became a craftsman; he bought a pewter cast and turned out small seals, otters, and buttons that he sold at the Anchorage Fur Rendezvous and smaller festivals. He carved flutes and learned to scrimshaw ivory, bone, and antlers. Anchorage shop owners sold his work. He liked to dress like an old-time trapper, often donning a buckskin coat, floppy hat, and medicine pouch.

Stavenjord had a questing intelligence and became an artistic, spiritual man. He was drawn to handicrafts; he learned how to carve flutes, then to play them and to write flute music. One friend told of hearing him play the instrument inside a tunnel on Anchorage's Coastal Trail, the haunting music echoing from the tunnel walls.

Paul and Peggy both loved black-powder shooting, the ancient form of riflery using muzzle-loaders. Paul joined a group of black-powder hobbyists called the McKinley Mountain Men and ran a black-powder shoot at the Trapper Creek Cabin Fever Reliever, an annual celebration of fading winter. One year he journeyed to the Fur Rendezvous and won a competition for the best pre-1840 costume.

"It was exciting," Peggy said later. "It was the Alaskan dream of living in the Bush. Some people go into the Renaissance period; we were attracted to the mountain man period." But the hardship and isolation wore on her. Their nearest neighbor was a mile away, the closest phone eight miles. When their son Josh was born in 1984, Peggy pushed Paul to move to a place where the children could go to school. They bought a cabin in Trapper Creek, a secluded place but located on a school bus route.

Stavenjord's thriving intellect drew him to spiritual gatherings. He met one of his friends at a Baha'i conference, another at a conference on shamanism; he presented a third with gifts of Hindu writings. Paul recorded and tried to sell compact discs of flute music, including one set of Native American tunes. He enjoyed teaching children, and he loved music and the wilderness.

Paul proved, however, to be a difficult husband and father. He left the railroad and took a job caring for special-education children. The cabin had no generator, so the family did without electricity or running water. Paul and Peggy separated in 1991 and Peggy filed for divorce, saying her husband had failed to support her emotionally or financially. She had supplemented their income by washing dishes and cleaning houses while he lost money working on his crafts.

Their split was relatively amicable and Paul stayed active in his children's lives. He found a girlfriend and moved to Georgia for a while, but moved back to remote Chulitna in early 1997 because he wanted to do more with his son. When a friend of his, Cheri Rapelye, visited him at his cabin a few months later, he gave her a card with an image of a beaver on the front. Inside was a short poem he had written about tenderness and peace. With it he presented a birthday cake, which he had made from scratch. "He was a perfect gentleman," Cheri said.

Rick Beery was a forty-eight-year-old electrician and jack-of-all-trades who lived in the Matanuska Valley community of Big Lake, north of Anchorage, where he worked at Fisher's Fuel. His wife, Deborah Rehor, was forty and a longtime customer service worker for Matanuska Electric Association. Rick was born in Alaska and left it only for a hitch in the U.S. Navy, serving two tours of duty in Vietnam. Debbie grew up near Denver, where she grew to love fishing and the outdoors. She married young, got divorced, and moved to be near her brother in Wasilla, Alaska, in 1977 with her four-year-old son. Though Rick was an avowed bachelor, he gave up that commitment when he met Debbie. They became a couple and had been together for about ten years, married for two.

Their principal home was in Big Lake, but they spent as much time as they could at their second home, a large cabin in Chulitna. Rick's dad had homesteaded the land there and Rick planned to retire on it some day. Debbie's son Chris was then nineteen and serving in Bosnia with the U.S. Army

People traveling to cabins in backcountry spots like Chulitna could be dropped off and picked up by the once-a-day train at flag stops, places where the engineer would stop when hailed by people standing beside the tracks. Rick and Debbie's getaway home was also eight miles from the Parks Highway, easily reachable on the four-wheeler all-terrain-vehicles they kept at the cabin.

The couple had sometimes complained of problems with their nearest neighbor, Paul Stavenjord, whose cabin lay about a mile distant. They told friends that Stavenjord had stolen fuel from their cabin. And when Rick sold the man a cellular antenna, Stavenjord also took a cable that was not part of the deal. Beery sent word through another neighbor that he wanted fifty dollars for the cable and Stavenjord returned it. Beery later found the cable had been cut to pieces.

Rick also suspected Stavenjord in the disappearance of a snowmachine and a .22 rifle from their cabin. Rick was a large man with a stubborn and sometimes gruff temperament; he was growing increasingly irritated by Stavenjord's thefts. Debbie was a slender redhead with a sweet disposition; her co-workers called her Sweetheart.

A long winter was finally coming to an end when Rick headed for his place at Chulitna on the Thursday before Memorial Day weekend in 1997. Debbie joined him the following day after she got off work. Debbie left her car at the highway and rode the eight miles to the cabin on the back of Rick's four-wheeler, her arms gripping his broad back throughout the bumpy trip.

Rick and Debbie were expected back at their jobs on Tuesday. When they failed to show up, Debbie's brother, Don Tidwell, headed north to check on them. He found their two dogs outside the cabin, which surprised him. Ordinarily they left the border collies inside when they left for a short trip. Tidwell thought perhaps they had bear trouble or got stuck on the far side of a river by rising water. He waited for them at the cabin, then on Wednesday he relayed a missing persons report through a friend to the Alaska State Troopers. The troopers launched a search and found Rick's body in a creek, two hundred yards from his four-wheeler and two miles from the cabin. He had been shot in the head.

Debbie and her red four-wheeler were missing. Their cabin had not been disturbed. Electrical workers installing fiber-optic cable along the railroad tracks told troopers they had noticed Rick's four-wheeler in the creek on both Saturday and Sunday, but they said it had been pulled out to dry land when they passed by again on Tuesday. The workers also mentioned that they had seen a recently used campsite near where the body had been found.

Since investigators found no sign of Debbie, she became a suspect in Rick's murder at first. But her friends scoffed at the notion, one saying: "Anyone who knew Rick and Debbie knows that is not even a remote possibility."

A young man phoned police, telling them he had been camping over the weekend near where Rick's body was found. He said he pulled the four-wheeler out of Pass Creek but did not notice the body. Police later said twenty-one-year-old Gavin Saha had slept just yards from Rick's corpse. He pulled the four-wheeler out of the creek and looked through a duffel bag attached to its luggage rack. Saha admitted taking a plastic bottle of Pepsi and a piece of gum but said he left everything else untouched.

With the murder unsolved and Debbie still missing, people living along the railroad grew increasingly nervous, many locking always-open doors and loading their guns. Jamie Miller, owner of the Igloo City gas station and store on the Parks Highway, said: "We left Anchorage to get away from the murder capital of Alaska. You can't run away from it anymore, but you still don't expect it in the middle of the wilderness."

Finally, a week after discovery of Rick's body, searchers found the remains of Debbie Rehor downstream in the same creek. Grass and tree limbs covered her body. She was naked from the waist down and her four-wheeler was not with the body. An autopsy showed she had had rough sex shortly before her death. Like Rick, she had been shot in the head.

Police at first considered Gavin Saha a suspect in the murders, but ruled him out when his DNA in hair and blood samples failed to match semen left in Rehor's body by her killer.

Saha was just one of several people asked to give samples for DNA comparison. Investigators had also become suspicious of the Beerys' nearest neighbor, Paul Stavenjord, whose account of his activities at the time of the shootings was not holding up well. He refused to give hair or fluid samples or allow a search of his cabin. When a State Trooper came by with a court order authorizing him to take a swabbing from the inside of Stavenjord's mouth, Paul complied, but took off from the cabin shortly after the officer left. Railroad workers who knew Stavenjord reported seeing him walking along the tracks. They said he had shaved off his beard and mustache. Then a security guard working near the railroad tracks saw him crash a red Honda four-wheeler into a bridge and take off running into the woods. It was Debbie Rehor's four-wheeler.

When DNA tests on Stavenjord's saliva matched the semen from Debbie's body, the troopers obtained warrants charging him with first-degree murder in both killings and with raping Debbie. Fliers showing Stavenjord with full beard and a computer simulation of his shaven face were distributed to police posts all along the Alaska road system, to the Canadian border crossing at Tok, and to Royal Canadian Mounted Police stations on the other side. They were posted in gasoline stations, restaurants, stores, boat launches, and campgrounds throughout the Talkeetna area. Even motorists driving the Parks Highway were handed copies.

In his cabin, police found a journal containing entries in which Stavenjord claimed he had met Debbie at the creek while he was out for a walk on that Friday of Memorial Day weekend. His notes said they talked and he played his flute for her, then they had romantic sex on the ground. He also claimed that she had called her husband on a cellular phone around 7:30 that night, a claim that was not supported by Debbie's telephone records. And Stavenjord had told investigators that he didn't own a small-caliber gun like the one used in the murders, but a neighbor said he had seen Paul carrying just such a gun a week before.

An intensive wilderness manhunt was then under way throughout the Chulitna area. Some troopers were stationed on mountaintops, some on bridges offering a long field of view. Others wearing camouflage clothing and face paint strapped extra pistols to their ankles and carried high-powered rifles, then went tree-to-tree through the dense underbrush. Their heavy armament was carried not just because of the risk from Stavenjord; the rugged country they were searching contained a healthy population of grizzly bears, which were then well into their summertime rambles.

Stavenjord's friends and family were dumbfounded by the accusations. The Paul they knew could not have committed such a crime. They speculated he might be innocent but that he ran away because he was under suspicion and feared his youthful criminal record would cause police to assume he was guilty. They hired one of Alaska's leading criminal defense attorneys, Carmen Gutierrez, who quickly issued a public plea for Paul to give himself up and not to hurt himself. Gutierrez gathered Paul's friends and family at a meeting to which she invited news reporters. All testified that he was a gentle man who could not have committed the murders. His ex-wife said: "Tell him that his family loves him, believes in him and to please come out safely so that we can get this cleared up."

The manhunt continued for a month, without results. Then on July 12, almost seven weeks after the shootings, Stavenjord called Gutierrez in Anchorage and said he was ready to give himself up. He met with her for several hours and then waited while she called a trooper friend. The long-missing fugitive was arraigned at the Anchorage courthouse and taken to jail. Gutierrez said he had wanted to come in to establish his innocence.

Stavenjord's surrender almost cost him his bit of national fame. The television show *America's Most Wanted* had been filming in Alaska and was about to broadcast his story. The producers decided to go ahead and run the segment anyway, despite the fact that he was no longer missing.

When Stavenjord finally told investigators about his travels during the massive hunt for him around Chulitna, he described how he had returned to his cabin the day after the manhunt began, then again after the search was ended. Nobody noticed. When he testified at trial the following year, Stavenjord said he had first eluded troopers by canoeing down Pass Creek to a camping spot. The next day he went back to his cabin and drove away on the stolen four-wheeler. When the security guard hailed him, he thought the man was a trooper and tried to flee. In the process he rolled the machine and ran away on foot, then hopped a slow-moving freight train out of the area. He rode a private shuttle van to Fairbanks, where he stayed for a week, then rode a van to Anchorage and later to Homer, where he camped for two weeks. Toward the end of the seventh week he took the shuttle back to the Chulitna area, hiked to his unguarded cabin, and stayed there for two more days. Finally he took the shuttle back to Anchorage and talked to a friend, who told him to call Gutierrez.

Stavenjord went on trial the following April in Palmer, south of Talkeetna, with Gutierrez and Jim McComas as his defense team. Like Gutierrez, McComas was one of Alaska's leading criminal lawyers. The lawyers argued that Rick Beery had come upon his wife and Stavenjord when Debbie was still half naked after the two had sex. They heard Beery's four-wheeler approach and scrambled for their clothes, the lawyers said, but it was too late. Gutierrez said Beery yelled at Stavenjord, shouting "I'm going to blow your fucking head off," then pulled out a gun and started shooting. She said Stavenjord dove to the ground, grabbed his .22 pistol from a vest pocket, and shot back at Beery, hitting him in the fore-head. When he looked around, Stavenjord saw Debbie lying on the ground, a bullet through her head. Beery had killed his own wife, the lawyer argued, and Stavenjord killed Beery in self-defense.

Gutierrez said Stavenjord panicked and decided police would never believe him, so he carried Debbie's body to a grassy spot down the creek and covered it with alder branches. Rick's body had floated into a deep pool, where Stavenjord left it. She said he picked up the spent bullet casings, threw them into a swamp, and tried to hide Rick's four-wheeler, but the machine got stuck in the creek, so he left it there. She denied that Stavenjord had stolen anything from Beery, saying he had bought the gun and put a down payment on Beery's snowmachine, taking it away with Rick's permission.

At the end of Stavenjord's testimony he played—at his lawyers' request—the flute melody he said he had played for Debbie just before her death. The lawyers argued that Stavenjord expressed himself better with music than he could with words. The judge sent the jury out of the courtroom while he played. Among his defense witnesses were an art dealer, a former girlfriend, and a woman who said she had asked Stavenjord to father her child because she was unable to conceive with her husband.

Prosecutor Bill Estelle dismissed Stavenjord's story of the shootings as "lies, lies, and more lies." At the end of a two-month trial, the jury convicted Stavenjord of two counts of murder. Several months later, before sentencing, Gutierrez and McComas asked to withdraw from the case, saying the attorney/client relationship had suffered a "total breakdown." They were replaced by a public defender who later sought a new trial for Stavenjord based on the argument that the defendant had lied in his testimony and that the two lawyers knew he was lying. The lawyers acknowledged that Stavenjord had lied to them about key points, but they said that at the time, they believed him. The public defender said Stavenjord's lies had prejudiced the jury against him. The new trial was denied.

Judge Eric Smith sentenced Stavenjord to 198 years in prison. The judge noted that his sentence took into account the fact that the murderer had never expressed any regret about the killings. The bodies of Rick and Debbie were cremated and the ashes scattered over Ruby Lake, their favorite fishing hole. It was a place where Debbie could catch fish when nobody else was getting a bite.

chapter eight

MANLEY HOT SPRINGS MURDERS

Michael Silka struck Manley Hot Springs residents as odd, but Manley often attracted characters looking for the end of the road, and Silka didn't seem violent or any more odd than some other visitors.

There were no witnesses to the seven murders at the boat launch in Manley Hot Springs. For a time, nobody knew that anybody had been killed at all. But some of the people going to the launch site that day were expected to return and none did. When neighbors began comparing notes, they began to worry.

When the events of May 17, 1984, were reconstructed, State Troopers determined that a lone and ill-tempered drifter from Illinois had shot and killed five men and one woman, dragged their bodies to the edge of the muddy Tanana River, and pitched them in. He also killed a two-year-old baby, but since the child's body was never found, it is still unknown whether he was shot like the rest or might have been thrown alive into the water.

Other victims of the same murderer included his next-door neighbor in Hopkinsville, near Fairbanks, and a State Trooper who was shot as he sat in the open door of a helicopter trying to apprehend the fleeing felon.

At age nineteen, Michael Silka was arrested twice in six weeks for walking around his Illinois hometown while carrying a primed muzzle-loading rifle. He had three similar weapons offenses on his record, as well as a burglary conviction. The police chief in the Illinois community of Hoffman Estates later told a newspaper reporter that young Silka had a passion for guns and considered himself a mountain man

He was one of three children and lived in a two-story brick home in the middle-class community near Chicago. The Hoffman Estates police chief said Silka came from a decent family, "basically nice people. He just turned out different."

Silka joined the Army after graduating from high school in 1977 and did a tour of duty at Fort Wainwright, near Fairbanks, as a helicopter mechanic. After his discharge, he returned to work in Alaska each summer. Just after Christmas of 1983, he showed up in Dauphin, Manitoba, Canada. He stayed at a Dauphin hotel through the winter, often wandering the streets. During his stay he built a cargo box atop his brown Dodge sedan, readying it for the long drive to Alaska.

Silka was sullen and unemployed but did not seem to lack for cash. He ate his meals in the hotel restaurant and didn't seem to drink or to be openly prone to violence. The owner of the Dauphin hotel noticed that the young man always had six or seven rifles and shotguns on the back seat of his car. His favorite was obviously a Rolling Block, a modern replica of a single-shot, large-caliber rifle used originally on the American frontier.

In early spring he drove on to Alaska and rented a small shack at Mile 4.7 of Chena Pump Road at the rural edge of Fairbanks. His was the cabin farthest back in the trees, one of a cluster of shacks and cabins in an area where neighbors were expected to mind their own business. The collection of cabins is called Hopkinsville.

One of his neighbors, a woman whose identity has been withheld from the public, found Silka hard to get to know and a bit threatening. On the afternoon of April 28, the woman had been chopping wood and talking to friend and neighbor Roger Culp when Silka walked by carrying a rifle. Silka stopped suddenly, picked up a large stick, and furiously bashed it against her chopping block, sending twigs and chips flying. "This is how you do it," he snarled, then turned and walked away.

The woman was frightened; the twenty-eight-year-old Culp was angry. When Culp started to follow Silka, she tried to talk him out of going. Culp said he would return in fifteen minutes. Shortly afterward the woman heard gunshots, at least eight, and Culp did not return.

Hopkinsville did not have telephone service, so the woman was unable to call police. She was too terrified even to walk the two hundred yards to the home of her landlord, Don Hopkins. Instead she hid in her cabin, a loaded shotgun by the door, and stayed there for two days.

At noon on the day after Culp disappeared, Wendy Hooker knocked on Silka's door. She wanted to confront him about a moose hide she suspected the newcomer had stolen. By his door, she noticed a small pool of blood. The blood did not surprise her; she assumed he had killed a small game animal. But then she circled to the back of the cabin and noticed a mound of freshly turned snow

covering a three-foot by six-foot mound. When she
wheeled to go back, Hooker noticed that her new footprints were filling up with fresh blood soaking up
through the snow.

Wendy knocked at the shack door again. Nobody
came and there was no noise from inside, but she had a
creepy feeling, a feeling she was being watched. Wendy
left hurriedly and told a friend about her experience,
then the two went to tell Don Hopkins. The friend, identified only as Tom, then went to Silka's cabin. Silka ran
out to meet Tom on the path, admitted he took the moose
hide, and promised to return it. Shortly afterward,
Hopkins walked up and the three men talked for several
minutes.

Wendy, Don Hopkins, and Tom were all suspicious
about what might have transpired at the Silka cabin.
They were unaware of Roger Culp's disappearance, but
Hopkins hadn't seen Culp lately and was beginning to
wonder. They gathered at Wendy's cabin and watched
to see if Silka drove off, but he didn't. Around five,
Hopkins left to call State Troopers and report their suspicions; Wendy and Tom left to go fishing.

But the message somehow became garbled. When
Trooper Mike Pullen and Fish and Game Protection Officer Paul Richards were dispatched to investigate, they
understood that both Michael Silka and Roger Culp had
disappeared and that neighbors suspected Culp might
have killed Silka. Both a trooper and a wildlife officer had
been dispatched since the two possible crimes, if any,
seemed to be either a homicide or a moose poaching.

While they drove, another officer ran a computer
check on the two names. Culp's showed a minor criminal record, including one violent incident, but Silka's
name came up clean. The investigators were unaware
that Silka was a new arrival in Alaska and that his record
was unblemished here, but Culp's record strengthened

their assumption that he was probably the perpetrator—
if any—and Silka would be the victim. Both officers were
tense as they pulled into Hopkinsville in a Fish and Game
vehicle. Richards tossed Pullen an extra set of car keys
and said, "If anything happens to me, you can get out of
here and get help."

They banged on the shack's door but heard only
silence. The officers walked behind the building and
found the reported mound in the snow. But to them it
appeared to be rounded, not oblong, and only about three
feet in diameter. They dug around in the snow, reaching
to ground level, but found only a buried and folded
moose hide. Another hide hung in a nearby tree.

The officers did not see the puddles of blood reported by Wendy Hooker, but they returned to the front
and did notice a small amount of blood near the door.
"It didn't look like anybody had been shot," Pullen said.
Still concerned about Silka's apparent disappearance and
possible murder, they pounded on the door once more.

A voice asked who was there. "I'm a State Trooper
and I want to talk to you," Pullen shouted.

"Are you alone?" the voice asked. Pullen answered
that he was not alone.

The door opened and Michael Silka stuck his head
and half his body through the door. Pullen could see
only one of Silka's hands. Though it appeared that there
had been no homicide and that Michael Silka was safe
at home, the two officers stayed and questioned Silka
for about five minutes. The man said he had been keeping some moose hides for hunter friends, had washed
blood from them, and was hanging them up to dry.

Silka's story seemed plausible and there was no
evidence of a crime, so the officers left. They didn't look
for Roger Culp since, if Michael Silka was unharmed,
there was no reason to pursue his neighbor, who had
not been seen since the previous day. But that could mean

anything, including the possibility that Culp had just gone into Fairbanks for the weekend.

Pullen later thought about the fact that Silka kept one hand out of sight while they talked at his cabin door. "The more I think about it," he said, "the more I know what was in the other hand."

Culp's woman friend was still hiding in her cabin, but apparently did not see the officers' car arrive and had spoken to no one since Culp stormed off toward Silka's shack. She would remain hiding until Monday. For still-unexplained reasons, she did not tell the story of Culp's disappearance publicly for nine days, when Don Hopkins drove her to trooper headquarters in Fairbanks.

A warrant was then issued and officers searched the ground around Silka's shack, which seemed abandoned. He had last been seen when Hopkins drove the woman witness to Fairbanks. Silka had summoned a tow truck to pull his car from the Hopkinsville mud, and then disappeared.

Investigators spent two days combing the then snow-free grounds around the shack. They brushed away patches of peat that appeared to have been placed there to cover something. Beneath were spots of red. Samples were sent to the state crime laboratory in Palmer and on May 16 the lab reported that the samples were definitely human blood. The report came back just one day before the carnage at Manley Hot Springs.

Bob Gentleman saw Silka's brown Dodge parked on the Elliott Highway thirty miles east of Manley on May 11, at a place where there was no obvious reason for stopping. Gentleman was visiting from Fairbanks and was headed for Minto with two Manley friends, Pat Burke and Heidi Heidtke. They discussed stopping to offer help, but Burke suddenly had a horrible feeling about the Dodge. Normally a fearless man, Burke shouted "Speed up! Don't stop!" Bob stomped on the gas pedal while Pat and Heidi peered at the Dodge as they rolled past. Both saw two passengers sitting with Silka, one of them a woman.

The Rev. Perry Hart of Minto came across Silka on the highway the next day. Hart warned the young traveler against going to Manley because he had heard the road was washed out, but Silka seemed somewhat irrational and intent on going anyway. The minister felt a sense of danger about the traveler and reached under his seat to make sure his weapon was still in its accustomed place.

Silka showed up in Manley Hot Springs on Mother's Day, May 13. He struck some people as odd—one later described him as "a real looney-tune"—but Manley is a tiny fishing and mining community and had always attracted people looking for the end of the road. He didn't seem violent or much weirder than some of their occasional visitors.

But Silka was definitely weird. He told some people he had come to fish for bass and muskie—species unknown in Alaska waters—and said he could smell clams in six feet of water. Dorothy Zoller ran into him at the Manley boat landing, near where he was camping. He had a seventeen-foot aluminum canoe atop his car and a large Bowie knife in a sheath. Silka talked to her about staking a homestead on the Zitziana River and using his military service to acquire bonus points toward the staking of free land. "He was really nice looking, except for his beard and hair," she said. "His shirt was off and he looked fit and muscular."

Not all Manleyites agreed on Silka's appearance, however; Sabie Gurtler described him as "nasty looking." Dorothy Zoller ran into him several times that week. Sometimes the man was talkative; sometimes he said nothing. On Thursday he was working silently on an Evinrude engine, which he had earlier said he planned to mount on the canoe. Silka walked up to her, appeared to be about to speak, then turned and walked away.

Between noon and two-thirty on Thursday, seven people went to the landing a quarter-mile from the village. Joe McVey and his good friend Dale Madajski went there to launch McVey's boat. Albert Hagen Jr. drove up with a load of brush. Fred Burk motored down the river from an upstream camp, planning to fix the clutch on his truck, which was parked in Manley. Also happening by were Lyman Klein, his pregnant wife Joyce, and their two-year-old son Marshall.

McVey, thirty-eight, was a wounded Vietnam veteran who sometimes wore metal leg braces. He and his wife kept a dozen sled dogs at their camp across the river from Manley. Dale Madajski was twenty-four and lived with his wife, Kirstin, on nearby Baker Creek. Hagen was a twenty-seven-year-old Athabascan who had recently returned to Manley after ten years fishing off the coast of California.

Fred Burk, known to his friends as Weeds, was a thirty-year-old trapper and member of a large and extended Athabascan family from Nenana. Lyman Klein was thirty-six and Joyce Klein was thirty. The Kleins were relative newcomers to the area, having arrived about two years previously. They were trying to decide whether to move upriver to the Kantishna district.

The boat launch was a popular spot, especially when the ice went out on the river and the water boiled with visible power. At least one Manleyite flirted unknowingly with fate that day. Bob Lee, postmaster and owner of the Manley Roadhouse, started for the landing about two. He was looking for a stove fitting he thought he could find at an old fish plant near the landing, but his friend Al Hagen waved from his yard when Bob's truck passed. As they talked, Al said he had such a fitting in his shop. He retrieved it and passed the ninety-eight-cent part to Bob through the truck window.

Hagen waved as his son Albert Jr. drove by with a pickup load of brush, headed for the landing and his own fate. Bob Lee turned around and headed back to the roadhouse. On the way home, he passed Lyman Klein, his wife, and their baby, who were motoring toward the landing on their four-wheeler.

Around 4:00 p.m. Sabie Gurtler drove to the landing with a carload of kids who wanted to watch the river. The place seemed deserted, though she noticed Silka's canoe was half-on and half-off his car. Near six she came back again and the canoe was gone.

When none of the seven returned from the landing, people began to worry. Alice McVey, Joe's wife, went to the river and found her husband's boat still there. A six-pack of beer was sitting in his truck. Alice knew Joe to forget and occasionally leave things behind, but going off without his beer seemed unlikely. Kirstin Madajski wondered what was keeping her husband Dale. But the weather had been unusually warm and pleasant, so perhaps the missing friends and relatives had just gone off somewhere. When day turned to night, then to morning, the worry intensified. About noon on Friday, Alice McVey called troopers in Fairbanks, who noted the report but felt there was no evidence of a mishap at that point. The overdue people could be on an outing.

The friends and families of the missing gathered at the Hagens' home. Somebody went to the landing and saw the stranger's car. Fearing that he might be missing too, they called his auto license number in to troopers. It matched the plate of Silka, who was by then being sought in the disappearance and possible murder of Roger Culp in Fairbanks. A trooper told people in Manley to be on guard and that officers would be there as soon as possible.

Troopers started arriving at 2:00 a.m. and began an aerial search in the early morning twilight, looking for Silka and any sign of the missing seven. At the boat launch they found massive blood spatters and drag marks, indicating people may have been shot and thrown into the fast-flowing river.

By Saturday afternoon, more than fifteen troopers were involved in the search, including five members of the Special Emergency Response Team, a force equipped with automatic weapons, wearing combat gear and specially trained for high-risk operations. Their air support included two helicopters and a SuperCub, a single-engine plane able to move fast, fly low, and land in tight spots. Meanwhile boats were combing the river below Manley, looking for bodies.

Lieutenant John Meyers was in charge of the SERT troopers until Captain Don Lawrence arrived from Fairbanks and announced he was taking command of the team. Meyers later reported that he complained because Lawrence didn't have the proper training or equipment to work with his team and that giving him a seat on a helicopter would require leaving one of his trained men behind. But Lawrence was adamant and climbed into the copter.

About three that afternoon, the SuperCub pilot reported that he had spotted a man far up the Zitziana River, an upstream tributary of the Tanana. The man was in a green, flat-bottom riverboat—Fred Burk's boat—and towing a loaded canoe. The pilot had made a low pass and got a good look at the man; it was Silka. The search team hurriedly broke off a rest stop at Manley and the helicopter pilots removed the doors from their aircraft.

The two choppers took off and headed for the Zitziana at treetop level, the SERT marksmen strapped into the two left seats, front and back. When the first chopper reached the area where Silka had been reported seen, the lead pilot spotted an open space where he could land and allow the SERT team to search the area on foot. The pilot swung around, approaching into the wind. Captain Lawrence wanted Silka to surrender, if possible, or at least to draw him out of hiding. He ordered pilot Tom Davis to hover while he shouted into the trees below with the copter's bullhorn. Davis told Meyers that he was thinking that he had made it through the Vietnam War, but now this captain was going to get him killed.

As the copter neared the clearing and slowed, Silka jumped from behind a tree, raised the big single-shot rifle, and fired two quick shots at the aircraft's open back door, reloading rapidly between shots. Trooper Troy Duncan saw Silka emerge and raised his own rifle, but found his radio headset interfered with the shot. Silka fired as Duncan scrambled to remove the earphones. The massive bullet hit Duncan in the head, killing him instantly. The second bullet struck the helicopter just inches from a spot that would have sent it crashing to the ground. Trooper Jeff Hall fired a long burst from his M-16 and cut Silka down, ending the man's murder spree and his life. Hall was grief-stricken; Troy Duncan had been one of his best friends.

Pilot Davis said later that Silka had set a trap for them. The murderer was a former soldier and knew that the helicopter would likely land in the open space in front of his hiding place and would have to approach by flying into the wind. "He was definitely aiming for the gunner position," the pilot said, "just like you would on a helicopter gunship."

Troopers met with the townsfolk that evening to try to pin down for certain the number and names of those missing. The Manley residents quickly narrowed the list to seven. They tried to guess what happened that afternoon by the riverbank. The most likely scenario was that Silka had argued with one or two of the men, lost his temper, and shot them. The others showed up while he was dragging the first bodies to the river. He apparently shot each in turn and threw them into the churning brown water.

The victims' friends, family, and neighbors spent weeks searching the river. Some volunteers spent weeks and months scouring the brush-choked banks. One at a time, most of the dead turned up, some within a mile of the Manley boat landing, another fifty miles downstream, the others in between. By the end of summer, the bodies of all but Joyce Klein, her toddler son Marshall, and Albert Hagen Jr. had floated to the surface and were recovered. The remains of the final three were never found, nor was the body of Roger Culp, who disappeared from Hopkinsville. Trooper Lieutenant John Myers told a newsman that hopes for finding the rest were slim. "This river doesn't give up its bodies very often," he said.

The officers involved in the search and gunfight were shocked by the bloody killings. One of the hardest things to accept was the murder of little Marshall Klein.

Investigator Jim McCann described the thoughts he and his teammates were having when they reached the boat launch and the enormity of what had happened hit them. "We just sat there and I tried to imagine what it was like . . . a two-year old kid. We knew he (Silka) was ours if he came back . . . a two-year old kid."

"I'm glad they shot the son of a bitch!" one towns-man said. Others took out their anger on Silka's car, de-stroying it where it sat near the blood-covered boat land-ing and pushing the wreckage into the river. Bob Lee now treasures the fitting that kept him away from the landing that day and probably saved his life. It still sits atop the Manley Roadhouse stove, where he placed it that day.

Media everywhere carried news about the mass murder. An article in a New York tabloid bore the head-line "Frontier Cops Whack Wilderness Weirdo."

At the request of his father, Michael Silka's ashes were buried in the National Cemetery in Sitka. The sur-vivors in Manley were furious, but Silka had been hon-orably discharged from the Army and was entitled to be buried in a military cemetery at government expense, no matter what he did in the years after his service.

The total number of Silka's victims is unknown. In addition to the nine about whose death there is no doubt, many people wonder about the two passengers seen in Silka's car on May 11. Though numerous witnesses said they saw three people in the car, and a restaurant cook said Silka and two hitchhikers stopped at his Livengood restaurant two days earlier, troopers concluded that the witnesses might actually have seen only piles of cloth-ing and gear stacked on the car seat. But some Manleyites suspect there are two more bodies out there somewhere, still uncounted.

chapter nine

HAVING TROUBLE
WITH GIRLS

---

*Police requests for tips about suspicious people
brought 7,000 phone calls. Most were from
Fairbanks residents concerned about weird neighbors—and in Fairbanks having weird neighbors
was not uncommon.*

Thomas Richard Bunday had been killing women
for almost two years before police realized they were
looking for a serial murderer. At first the cases were just
young women reported missing, a cause for concern but
not all that unusual. Then bodies began turning up and
the disappearances got a closer look.

There were clues, but nothing definitive. A task force
sorted through thousands of leads, and Bunday's name
occasionally popped up, but a faulty FBI profile of the likely
killer kept turning them in other directions. By the time
Bunday's name registered as the prime suspect, he was long
gone from Alaska. But a talented and dogged team of homicide detectives tracked him down in Texas, confronted
him—at first unsuccessfully—then ran an elaborate scam
that resulted in his confession, and the solution of one of
the worst crime series ever reported in Alaska.

Glinda Sodemann, age nineteen, was last seen near her home on August 29, 1979. She was a newlywed and daughter of an Alaska State Trooper, an unlikely candidate for a disappearance of her own choosing. Her husband Jerry reported her missing, but the initial investigation turned up nothing. There seemed to be little going on in her personal life to suggest she had run away, but neither was there any evidence to suspect anything else.

Glinda's decomposed body was found the following October in a gravel pit near Moose Creek on the Richardson Highway outside Eielson Air Force Base, twenty-two miles south of Fairbanks. She had been shot in the face with a pistol of approximately .38-caliber, but the condition of the body prevented investigators from determining whether she had been raped. When a married woman is found murdered, suspicion often centers first on the husband and State Troopers did question Jerry Sodemann, but he was quickly cleared.

On June 11, 1980, Doris Oehring's older brother Thomas saw his eleven-year-old sister on Badger Road in North Pole, a suburb of Fairbanks, sitting astride her bicycle and talking to a stranger in a bluish car. The man was wearing blue clothing that looked a lot like an Air Force uniform. Two days later, Doris disappeared and her bicycle was found hidden in bushes along Badger Road. A witness reported seeing a small, bluish car come racing out of a roadside turnout about the time that Doris went missing.

Young Thomas Oehring gave a description of the man to a police artist, who developed a composite sketch for distribution to police agencies and news media. State Troopers asked Eielson Air Force Base security police for a list of cars registered to drive on base and matching the descriptions of the two cars, which might or might not have been the same vehicle. The Air Force came back with a list of 550 names and license plates. Bunday's name was on the list, but he was just one of 550, with nothing to make him stand out from the rest. Bunday—who was known by the name Richard Bunday—lived in Moose Creek, a few miles from where Glinda Sodemann's body was found.

Troopers also asked other police agencies and the public for help, the plea bringing in a massive pile of suggestions but no leads pointing at a specific suspect. Doris Oehring's disappearance was highly suspicious and seemed likely to have involved kidnapping, if not murder, but real clues to her whereabouts were very much lacking.

On January 31, 1981, the family of twenty-year-old Marlene Peters reported her missing. She was last seen trying to hitch a ride from downtown Fairbanks to Anchorage, where her father was ill with cancer. The State Trooper investigator assigned to look into the report assumed Marlene's was a routine missing persons case. Though her family was anguished and foul play was suspected, there was no evidence linking the disappearance to any other unsolved crimes in the agency's files. There was no body and no clue to what had happened to her. And if she were hitchhiking to Anchorage when she disappeared, whatever mishap she encountered could have occurred anywhere along the three-hundred-mile route.

Then just five weeks after Marlene's disappearance, sixteen-year-old Wendy Wilson dropped out of sight. She was last seen hitchhiking and climbing into a light blue pickup truck in Moose Creek. Wendy's vanishing led police to believe they might have a serial killer at work and that the various disappearances of young women might be related. Just three days later, Wendy's body was found near Johnson Road, near the trans-Alaska pipeline and thirty-two miles south of Fairbanks. She had been strangled and her face destroyed by a shotgun blast.

Nine weeks after Wendy Wilson's body was found, the remains of Marlene Peters turned up just two miles away on Johnson Road. Like Wendy, Marlene had been strangled and her face torn by shotgun pellets, virtually obliterating her features. And two days after Marlene's remains were identified, the Fairbanks Police Department was notified that nineteen-year-old Lori King was missing. Lori was last seen walking in Fairbanks and may have been hitchhiking.

With the body count and list of missing women mounting, publicity on the cases intensified and the killings became known as the Fairbanks Serial Murders. Police, the military, and civilian volunteers launched a massive search of the Johnson Road area, looking for any sign of Lori King and Doris Oehring, and any clues to the murders of the two women whose bodies were found near there. Investigators asked the public to report any possible clues, any suspicious activities they saw, and any strange people showing up in their neighborhoods. One police officer urged people to write down the license number of any car seen picking up a hitchhiker. "Write it down; throw it in the glove compartment," he said, "and then call it in to State Troopers."

Then, on September 2, four airmen on a rabbit hunt stumbled across the body of Lori King in a wooded area near an old Nike missile site off Johnson Road, a section that had been missed by the earlier searchers. Like the others, Lori had been strangled and her face shattered by a shotgun blast. Since her body lay on a federal reservation, the FBI joined the case and an Area-wide Homicide Task Force was formed to manage and prioritize the growing number of leads and to follow up on the most promising ones. The task force included Alaska State Troopers, the FBI, the Eielson Air Force Base Office of Special Investigations, the Army's Criminal Investigation Division from Fort Wainwright, the Fairbanks Police Department, and the North Pole City Police Department.

State Trooper Investigator Sam Barnard flew to Atlanta, Georgia, where a joint federal and state task force was investigating the serial murders of young black men. The probe had turned up a massive number of leads and tips. Barnard studied how the Atlanta task force used relatively new computer technology to manage the avalanche of information, sorting the leads out by value, matching those that seemed to have relevance to each other, and deciding which leads to follow and how.

Later Barnard flew to the FBI Behavioral Sciences Division in Quantico, Virginia, and met with experts there. Barnard spent two exhausting days being quizzed by a team of three FBI psychologists and psychiatrists. He gave the behavioral wizards the details of the Fairbanks killings and they developed a profile of the likely murderer.

The experts said the serial killer was probably single, lived alone, had a hard time holding a job, and was a civilian. Barnard took the profile back to Alaska and distributed it to everyone involved in the investigation. Since the Quantico experts have a success rate of about eighty-five percent, and since their profile of the Atlanta murderer proved right on target, the profile of the Alaska serial killer was given great credence by the Fairbanks task force. Barnard found the process exhausting but went away feeling that he at last had something solid to work with.

The investigators sought other expert help as well, including a psychologist who suggested that the murderer's primary motive might not have been sexual, though some of the victims had been raped. By shooting the women in the face, especially those whose features were obliterated by shotgun blasts, the murderer might have been trying to wipe out their identities. He might, in fact, be trying to wipe out the identity of someone else, someone whose face he saw in his mind when he pulled the trigger. And the shootings seemed overkill since the victims had already been strangled before the gun was fired.

Police requests to the public for tips on suspicious people and activities brought massive numbers of calls and potential leads of all kinds, more than seven thousand in all. Most of the tips proved to be reports by Fairbanksans concerned about their weird neighbors—and in Fairbanks having weird neighbors was not uncommon. With the 550 names supplied by the Eielson Office of Special Investigations and a thousand more offered by volunteers, the investigative task force needed a thoughtful way to sort, prioritize, and deal with them, as Barnard had seen done in Atlanta.

Trooper Chris Stockard was a self-described techno-geek with computer training. He was assigned to work with Trooper Sergeant Jim McCann, one of the most capable, dedicated, and creative homicide detectives ever to work in Alaska. McCann had become one of the lead investigators on the team. Together McCann and Stockard would pursue the murderer far beyond Alaska's borders. Under Stockard's supervision, all of the thousands of pieces of information assembled in the two and a half years of investigation were entered into state computers, an effort that ran around the clock for three months. Then Stockard cross-referenced items in the new database, finding ways to reduce the really valuable leads to a manageable number and looking for clues suggesting a closer look at some candidates.

The task force came close to identifying the murderer in February 1982 when a special agent in Eielson's OSI reported that he had identified three persons working on the Air Force base who acted strangely toward women. One of the three was thirty-three-year-old Technical Sergeant Richard Bunday, an electrical expert who had demonstrated what was described as "inappropriate behavior around female co-workers and had generally showed disrespect for members of the female sex." One woman who worked with him said Bunday was verbally abusive and she was afraid of him. But Bunday didn't fit the FBI profile in its most important predictions. He was weird enough—as, so it seemed, were thousands of Fairbanksans—but Bunday was married, had children, and held a regular job in the Air Force. The airman was kept on the list of prospects, but many others who displayed bizarre behavior seemed far more promising and likely to be the real killer.

The last known murder had occurred on May 16, 1981. By November 1982 the task force concluded that whoever had killed the women was either dead, imprisoned on an unrelated charge, or had left the area. And, they decided, those who moved away would include military personnel transferred outside the state. The team began an intensive review of each of the four murders as well as the disappearance and assumed murder of Doris Oehring, and a sixth killing whose details didn't quite match the others. The sixth case was the killing of Cassandra Goodwin, a twenty-two-year-old woman whose body was found September 16, 1980, off the Parks Highway near Hurricane Gulch. The investigative team asked the Air Force for a list of all military personnel who had transferred from Eielson after Lori King was shot in the face. They also asked fifty police agencies and the OSI to report any murders similar to those in Alaska that occurred near Air Force installations anywhere in the world.

The Air Force came back with a list that included the name of Sergeant Richard Bunday, who had transferred out on September 9, 1981, a week after Lori's body had been found. Bunday had transferred to Sheppard Air Force Base near Wichita Falls, Texas—and a murder much like those near Fairbanks had been recently reported there. The Alaska task force questioned Bunday's Alaska friends, neighbors, and co-workers. Most considered him a loner and didn't particularly like him. The investigators also noticed that Bunday's facial features were a lot like the composite picture drawn by the artist from the description Thomas Oehring gave of the man he saw talking to his sister two days before she disappeared.

The team further found that Bunday had two vehicles registered in his name that roughly fit the descriptions given by witnesses. Bunday owned several guns, including a .357 magnum pistol and several shotguns. His work and recreational habits sometimes took him to the areas where the bodies were found. One young woman said Bunday tried to pick her up once; another said he followed her numerous times.

With information about Bunday accumulating rapidly, Trooper Sergeant Sam Barnard hopped on another airplane in January 1983 and flew to Sheppard Air Force Base. There he interviewed Bunday, who seemed cooperative and answered Barnard's questions. But the suspect refused to take a lie-detector test or to allow a search of his home or even to give samples of his hair. Though Bunday's refusals seemed suspicious, both he and his wife were considered somewhat bizarre individuals and his refusal was not surprising.

Bunday's parents had what his brother Ralph called a "tumultuous marriage." The parents often fought when young Richard was growing up in Tennessee, and the father often beat him. In fact, Richard received a beating just the day before the father died. Richard skipped the funeral and went to a band contest in Nashville.

Richard met his future wife while in high school and joined the Air Force after their marriage. He was eventually assigned to Eielson Air Force Base in Alaska. A longtime Air Force friend reported that Bunday was "friendly, joking, good natured." Bunday's wife, Marcia, later told police they had been having marital difficulties but were working through them. But Ralph said Richard occasionally called him from Alaska and sounded depressed.

During their research, the investigative team learned that both Bunday and his wife were something other than average people. Richard had been in the Air Force for sixteen years and was previously stationed in Southeast Asia. During that time, he had an affair. When Marcia found out, she started an affair of her own and became pregnant by her lover. One of the Bundays' two children, a son, resulted from Marcia's extramarital fling. Though the relationship of Richard Bunday to the son of his wife's lover is unknown, the teenage boy's bedroom was spartan and almost military-like in appearance. The younger daughter's room was colorful, somewhat messy and a typical child's room. While in Fairbanks, Marcia had experimented with different re-

ligions, adopting each for a few months before dropping it in favor of another.

A high school friend reported that Bunday was a
practical joker with a sadistic streak. Bunday liked to
sneak up on people and pinch them on the chest hard
enough to leave black and blue spots. He once had a
months-long feud with a neighboring farmer. Richard
claimed the farmer hurt one of his pets. To get even,
Bunday put cherry bomb firecrackers in baby food jars,
then threw them at the farmer's livestock. When the
firecrackers exploded, the jars became shrapnel bombs.

During the Fairbanks murder spree, Bunday started
going to see a military psychologist because of marital
difficulties. Bunday visited Clarence Williams, chief of
the Eielson mental health clinic, six times during that
period. The psychologist later went to prison for hiring
a hit man to shoot his twenty-five-year-old wife in the
face with a shotgun in November 1980. Captain Williams hoped to collect on a large insurance policy and
was trying to make his wife's murder look like one of
those in the unsolved serial murder cases, not knowing
that his patient was the killer.

Williams told a *Fairbanks Daily News-Miner* reporter in a telephone interview from his prison cell that
Bunday "had a lot of unresolved problems concerning
his father. He resented the fact his father died. There
were feelings that his father died before he could prove
he was somebody. There was a lot of love/hate."

While Sam Barnard was in Texas, the Fairbanks
team showed Bunday's photograph to people living near
the murder scenes and asked Doris Oehring's older
brother to view a photo lineup that included Richard
Bunday's face. "That's him," the boy said. Young Oehring

said that beyond any doubt, Bunday was the man he had seen talking to his sister two days before her disappearance. In Texas, Barnard told Bunday that the Oehring boy had identified his photo, but Bunday did not react to the information. Barnard flew back to Alaska feeling that the evidence was inconclusive and concerned that Bunday did not fit the FBI profile that he had so laboriously helped develop at Quantico.

The task force, however, decided it was time to investigate Bunday more closely. On March 7, 1983, McCann and Stockard flew to Texas and began three days of work with Texas and federal police officials, including the Air Force's Office of Special Investigations. They shared information and made plans for OSI to place a loose twenty-four-hour surveillance on Bunday once contact was made with him. McCann and Stockard rented two rooms at the La Quinta Motel and staged one to look like a long-used stakeout headquarters. They borrowed filing cabinets from the military base and put up calendars with days and weeks crossed off, making it look like they had been working there for several months. The troopers filled trash cans with crushed coffee cups and pasted up phony surveillance photos and notes to call nonexistent colleagues. This elaborate stage was set up at the far end of the motel room, where a visitor could see them only from a distance. Then they called Bunday and asked him to drop by.

When Bunday showed up, McCann and Stockard introduced themselves and gave the airman their business cards. McCann is a master at making friends with suspects and suggested to Bunday that he and Stockard were the final shift in a long surveillance and were there to wrap things up, to tie down a few of the details that were still a little fuzzy. Bunday spent two hours with the Alaska detectives that day and agreed to return the following day. During his stay, he answered their questions with rather vague responses, but he notably did not deny killing the women near Fairbanks. At one point he admitted: "I had trouble with girls in Alaska."

Bunday arrived at the La Quinta the next day within fifteen seconds of the agreed time, as he had on the previous day. This time McCann and Stockard were more accusatory, telling him they knew that he had killed the Alaska women; they knew how and when, but they just didn't know why. They told him details of the crimes and why they were sure he had done them. It was time to clear up the remaining questions, they said; time to get everything on the table. And since Bunday had now killed a Texas woman, he was certain to be spending many years of his life in prison. Either the Texas Rangers or Alaska State Troopers were sure to nail him for murder, one or the other. The troopers told him he might prefer to confess and spend those years in a prison located in a cool climate rather than in a hot and smelly Texas cell. Again he listened quietly, gave short answers, and did not deny involvement in the murders. By the end of the four-hour interview, the suspect was crying and appeared close to confessing.

Bunday agreed to return again next day and did so, once again arriving within seconds of the agreed meeting schedule. This time he didn't stay. He handed the troopers a note, carefully avoiding eye contact, and departed. The note contained a weak denial that he had been involved in the murders. It was time to search his home and vehicles. The next day, Sunday, March 13, McCann and Stockard went to the suspect's residence carrying search warrants and accompanied by an FBI agent, a representative of the Wichita Falls district attorney's office, and observers from the Sheppard OSI.

The searchers spent more than twelve hours combing through Bunday's home and vehicles. They were looking for hair and fibers, guns, ammunition, clothing items, and mementos of the murders. They went away with bags of material, including ammunition of the type used in the murders, a scrapbook containing newspaper clippings about the Alaska murders and the investigation, and surveillance-type photos of young girls.

Though the officers didn't realize it at the time, Bunday's car keys had been dropped into one of the bags. An hour after the officers left his home, Bunday called and asked about the keys. McCann was in the shower; he stepped out and stood naked and dripping, talking to the suspect. He quickly looked through the materials they had collected, found the car keys, and apologized for the mistake. He said they would return the keys when they met next. But McCann felt Bunday was getting ready to confess. McCann stood there, still naked, trying to keep the suspect talking. He asked about the Alaska murders again and found Bunday willing to talk and coming very close to admitting he had done them. Though still somewhat vague about the details on the others, Bunday specifically denied murdering Cassandra Goodwin. He told McCann that the team should be looking for somebody else in Alaska for that killing. They agreed to meet again the following morning.

This time there was no seconds-to-spare, on-time arrival. Bunday had agreed to be at the La Quinta at nine in the morning but knocked on the door at eight, catching the troopers by surprise. They recovered and surreptitiously turned on their tape recorder, which was hidden under the bed. Bunday declined to enter the room. He stood in the doorway and admitted to murdering the five women in Alaska, including the still-missing Doris Oehring. He said her body could be found in a remote area of Eielson Air Force Base. When the tape recorder reached the end of a reel, Bunday heard the tape flapping, realized his discussion was being recorded, and started to leave. McCann and Stockard had no authority to arrest anyone in Texas, and Texas police couldn't arrest him for crimes committed in Alaska without a warrant, so they let him go. Bunday agreed to appear again the next morning, giving the troopers time to obtain the paperwork needed before they could finally collar their murderer.

They were waiting with proper warrants on Tuesday, but Bunday failed to show up. They called his house and were told by Marcia Bunday that her husband was out riding his motorcycle. He was scheduled to meet her that afternoon at one o'clock at the local H&R Block office to work on their tax return. The OSI surveillance team followed Bunday to the tax preparer's office but, when the Bundays' appointment ended, the team mistakenly followed Marcia in her car instead of Richard, who roared away in another direction on his motorcycle.

McCann and Stockard waited in frustration at their motel room, ready to put handcuffs on Bunday as soon as they could find him. Later that afternoon they received a dreaded telephone call. In the midst of a Texas gully-washer rainstorm, Bunday had stopped his motorcycle under an overpass. He pulled the two troopers' business cards from his pocket and placed them carefully on a rock. Then he raced off down the highway until he saw a twelve-wheel dump truck approaching in the opposite lane. Bunday swerved across the centerline and bore in on the dump truck. The startled driver turned away from the collision, but the motorcyclist literally chased him across the highway and smashed into the truck just behind the cab. Bunday was killed instantly.

The investigators later determined that hairs found in Bunday's pickup truck came from Wendy Wilson and that shotgun shells found in the Bunday home were from the same manufactured batch as the shells used to destroy the faces of Lori King and Wendy Wilson. After several searches, the bones of eleven-year-old Doris Oehring were found two years later, scattered over a remote section of Eielson Air Force Base. Bunday had apparently murdered her at one of his favorite killing spots and then driven through the Eielson gate with the girl's body in his trunk, presumably being waved through by a military policeman guarding the base entrance. The method of the girl's murder could not be determined, though Bunday had said he strangled her.

Despite the evidence and the circumstances, a Texas coroner refused to rule that Bunday had committed suicide. It was apparently an accident, he said. And Texas Rangers told the Alaskans that the boyfriend of the murdered Wichita Falls woman was a drug dealer and the prime suspect in that case, even though she had been shot in the face and the crime closely resembled the Alaska cases. No arrest was ever made, leaving McCann and Stockard convinced that Bunday had committed the Wichita Falls murder and denied it solely to avoid spending the rest of his life in a Texas prison. Before he decided on suicide, they thought, a cell in Alaska probably seemed preferable.

Stockard was later called to testify in a Texas civil suit. Marcia Bunday had sued her insurance company because it refused to pay double indemnity for her husband's death, which was officially listed as an accident. The insurance company refused to pay double the policy amount because Richard Bunday was a serial killer who appeared to have taken his own life. The insurance company is believed to have prevailed in the case.

When word of Bunday's death and the truth about the murders first reached Fairbanks, one man told a newspaper reporter: "He's lucky he's dead. It would have been better if they'd let the mothers have him."

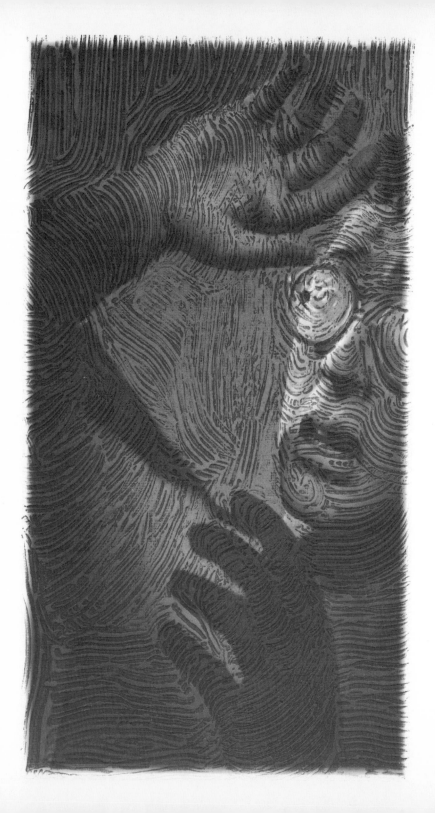

chapter ten

MURDER ON HIS MIND

Louis Hastings was a loner, but this didn't set him apart in McCarthy. Then he began hoarding guns, ammunition, a silencer, commando gear, and keeping a list of 200 Alaska political and civic leaders.

Louis Hastings was angry for a very long time, but nobody knew. He was an environmentalist, a man who loved small creatures and wild places. He once volunteered to clean birds soiled in an oil spill, and he hated the trans-Alaska pipeline, which he considered a violation of the natural world. Hastings was an intelligent, quiet man, and beneath his reserved exterior he despised people, despised what their overdevelopment and overpopulation were doing to Alaska's wilderness, which he considered his own. Hastings was a bearded and balding man known to environmental activists as one who shared their views. But his love for nature and its bounty masked his seething hatred for people, many people, and he kept a list.

Hastings tried to annihilate the people of McCarthy, a tiny unorganized community at the edge of one of Alaska's most beautiful wildernesses, the Wrangell-St. Elias National Park. No one knows exactly how many people were present in and around McCarthy that day. About two dozen made their year-round homes in the area, but half or more were generally away at any one time. What is clear is that Hastings shot all he could find, killing six and wounding two. Were it not for the exceptional courage and good luck of a few of his targets, he might have killed them all.

A psychiatrist later testified that Hastings was not insane but suffered from a personality disorder: he considered himself an exceptional person and valued his own ideas over those of other people. The murder spree was a cold and calculated act. He prepared himself to take human lives by shooting a rabbit, the first kill of his life.

Hastings claimed the killings were part of an elaborate plot in which he planned to kill the mail plane pilot and take her airplane. He would use the plane to dump all the bodies on the glaciers of the Wrangell Mountains. He planned to land on the highway and rig the plane to take off by itself, then disable the trans-Alaska pipeline with bullets, hijack a fuel tanker truck, and incinerate himself by smashing the tanker into a pipeline pump station. But the same psychiatrist doubted Hasting had such a plan, saying the man's inflated sense of self-worth would have prevented him from seriously considering such an end to his life.

Louis D. Hastings was born January 1, 1944, in Leewood, Kansas, a small suburb outside Kansas City. His mother and sister told a judge that Louis was a shy young boy who had a difficult father but became a gentle, caring person who was kind to the elderly, loving and patient with children, gentle with animals. His sister described their father as a master of psychological abuse, a man who returned from World War II in 1945 and was insensitive and disapproving toward his son, then just a year old. The father eventually left the family to make his way as a gigolo.

Young Louis suffered from chronic depression, though it seemed to respond to treatment. He served in the Air Force and became a computer programmer, but not a particularly good one. One of his few friends said Hastings always thought himself a better technician than he actually was. "Good programmers looked at his stuff and they weren't impressed," the friend said. "He was like all computer programmers, a little weird. But you have to be that way to be a programmer. You have to be into yourself. Lou didn't talk a lot. He was introverted. He seemed to do better with machines than with people."

Hastings worked for five years as a computer programmer at Stanford University, in Palo Alto, California, but remained introverted and rarely spoke of his past. His co-workers thought he seemed excessively worried about his personal safety. His off-work activities included volunteering with a California group to rescue seabirds soiled by oil spills. Hastings was appalled by the impact he saw on sea creatures from oil and the reckless works of man. He wanted to get away. In June 1979 he married Lennie Stoval, a Stanford librarian. The couple honeymooned in Alaska, staying for a time at Kennecott Lodge, a seasonal tourist facility in the remote and hauntingly beautiful setting of McCarthy. They decided to quit their jobs at Stanford and move to Alaska, which they did the following spring.

In Anchorage, Hastings drifted into the computer subculture and tried to start a business from his home, though the venture never prospered. Hastings found the relative sophistication of Anchorage too much like Palo Alto and longed for a purer life in a wilder place. He and his wife purchased a long-unoccupied house on the property of the old Kennecott Copper Corporation mine five miles from McCarthy. Louis and Lennie spent the summer of 1982 repairing and improving the old house.

The mine once exploited one of the world's largest copper lodes and employed more than a thousand people, rugged folk who lived and worked in the now-empty valley below. The copper lode was discovered in 1900 by prospectors who spotted a bright green patch on a mountain slope above Kennicott Glacier. They climbed up and took samples of a copper vein later determined to be ten to twenty times richer than most of the world's largest copper deposits. The prospectors named the mountain Bonanza Peak.

The find followed the discovery of gold on the Klondike River in the nearby Yukon Territory. That find triggered the Klondike Gold Rush and brought many kinds of mineral seekers to Alaska, sending prospectors swarming through the territory. The Bonanza Peak copper discovery fired the imagination of wealthy industrialists and touched off a competitive scramble by giant commercial syndicates to build a railroad to the site from Prince William Sound. Among them were the wealthy Guggenheim organization and J. P. Morgan, who joined forces, purchased the rights to the Bonanza Peak lode, and formed the Alaska Syndicate, which included the newly formed (and mis-

spelled) Kennecott Copper Corpoation and the Alaska
Steamship Company.

The syndicate's crews and those of their determined competitors came ashore in competing
camps at Katalla, Valdez, and Cordova and worked
feverishly to lay the first track from tidewater to the
mine and win priority transportation rights for the
ore. At one point, railroad workers clashed in a his-
toric gunfight in a ravine north of Valdez. Eventually
the Guggenheim/Morgan syndicate won out and 198
miles of rail linked the mine to the sea at Cordova.
The line was named the Copper River and Northwestern Railroad, completed in 1911 at a cost of nearly
$40 million. (Workers on the railroad included Rob-
ert Stroud, who later became known as the Birdman
of Alcatraz. See chapter 4.)

During its thirty-year history, the four deep shafts
of the Kennecott mine produced thousands of tons of
copper ore worth hundreds of millions of dollars.
McCarthy was one of four nearby communities where
mine workers and hangers-on lived. The town had a
peak population of about 650 and was the sin city of
the four, offering the miners a menu of hotels, broth-
els, and illegally distilled whiskey.

The mine was closed and abandoned in 1938,
when the Depression sank copper prices, leaving the
area to those people determined to live the wilderness life. Mostly they were individuals and couples
who valued their privacy and respected that of their
scattered neighbors, expecting such concern to be
mutual. By the time Louis Hastings arrived, their numbers were so small, said neighbor Nancy Gibert, "that
we know each other by our boot tracks. You walk out
for water and you say, hey, so-and-so's been by on the
path."

The few determined individualists living in and around McCarthy in 1983 gathered in small numbers when Lynn Ellis flew in with the mail every Tuesday from Glennallen. They mostly waited at the rustic home of Les and Flo Hegland, an older couple who provided weather reports to the Federal Aviation Administration and used their cabin as the unofficial post office. The Heglands took their responsibility seriously and added a heated porch where arriving packages could be kept out of the weather until their owners came by.

Maxine Edwards had lived there for twenty-five years with her husband Jim on a homestead across the Kennicott River, a homestead where she had home-schooled her two children. Her friends called her Maxine the Diligent because she could drive a bull-dozer in the afternoon, then serve dinner with linen and crystal in the evening. On the morning of March 1, Maxine crossed the frozen river pulling a small plastic sled to carry any packages brought by Lynn Ellis. She walked to the Hegland cabin, just off the McCarthy airstrip, and went in to join Les and Flo for her weekly visit in the warmth of their kitchen stove.

Bonnie Morris came by on a sled towed by her dog team to drop off some outgoing mail, but left right away. One of her dogs was going into heat and she needed to get home before the team became unmanageable. Bonnie invited Maxine to stop by for cookies, then shouted "Hike!" and her team headed for home.

Harley King was a hunting guide and former commercial fisherman living at Long Lake, twenty miles up the valley, home to him and his wife Jo since 1966. In the 1950s, Harley hunted wolves with fellow guide Jay Hammond, a self-described bushrat who later became governor of Alaska. Ordinarily Harley preferred to wait until after the flight arrived and drop by at his leisure to see if any mail had arrived for him or Jo. But that day he left early. Family friend Donna Byram planned to fly out on the mail plane and visit Anchorage, so Harley was going to pick Donna up at her cabin and carry her on a sled behind his brand new snowmachine, a Ski-Doo.

Young Tim and Amy Nash lived in a cabin four miles from the community. They were newlyweds, preferred to be alone, and weren't expecting any mail. Amy had come to McCarthy as a tourist the previous year and met Tim there. He was living alone after a divorce. The two fell in love, were married at Christmas, and had just returned on Valentine's Day from a long honeymoon in the East. When they returned, their neighbors gave them a quarter of a moose and a mincemeat pie with a heart carved into it.

Lynn Ellis was warming up his small airplane that morning at Glennallen Airport, preparing for the hourplus flight to McCarthy, 100 miles to the southeast. The owner and chief pilot of a small charter service, he was McCarthy's only direct link to the outside world. McCarthy was beyond the reach of electricity, telephones, and television. An unpaved road ended at the river, which was crossed in summer in an elevated cable car, pulled hand over hand. Lynn Ellis knew all of McCarthy's winter residents personally.

Louis Hastings was a loner and an oddball, but those traits did not set him apart in McCarthy; most of the winter residents of this remote village were eccentrics in one way or another. Hastings stayed away from most of the others, but nobody thought that unusual, not in their part of the country. By late winter of 1983,

Hastings' business and marriage were both in trouble. He spent quite a bit of time at his lonely cabin, but his wife Lennie was rarely there. Somewhere along the line, Hastings' mind rounded a corner and never turned back. He began hoarding guns, ammunition, a silencer, and commando gear, and keeping a list of two hundred of Alaska's political and civic leaders. The list included the phone numbers and home addresses of members of the Anchorage Police Department's Crisis Intervention Response Team, a squad of highly trained and heavily armed officers.

Hastings spent the evening of February 28 having a few drinks and playing a board game with his closest neighbor, Chris Richards, twenty nine, a summertime road construction worker and owner of a large and friendly husky. Richards and the dog lived in a cabin on a hillside above Kennicott Glacier. Hastings had already decided he would come for Richards first—when the time came—because the young man's cabin was just a mile down the glacier from his and was isolated. Hastings wanted to test a few things without having to deal with others before he was ready.

On the morning of March 1, Hastings left his small bedroom, hung a towel to dry on the fireplace, and headed down the glacier. He always met the mail plane, so Richards was not surprised when Hastings showed up outside his door about 8:30. Richards invited him in for coffee and was reaching for a cup when a bullet smashed through his eyeglass lens and tore into his eye. The noise was loud, but moments later he heard an even louder shot and felt a bullet tear a furrow in his neck. Richards fell to the cabin floor bleeding, stunned and shocked. He screamed and demanded Hastings stop shooting.

"You should see yourself," Hastings said. "You're down on the ground. You're already dead. Stay there and I'll make it easy for you."

Richards' surprise flashed into fear, then into rage. "I was suddenly goddamned mad," he said later. He jumped to his feet, wrestled with Hastings, and grabbed a butcher knife from a nearby table. Richards stabbed Hastings in the thigh and dove for the door, then churned through the snow toward the nearby trees, expecting at any moment to be shot in the back. He ran to the tourist lodge, found no one, and trotted off down the trail, adrenaline pumping. Hastings followed Richards' tracks to the lodge and set it afire, apparently hoping to trap Richards inside.

Hastings decided he was dissatisfied with his weapons. After being shot with Hastings' two pistols, Richards had gotten up and run away. Hastings decided to use a weapon with greater firepower, a .223 semiautomatic rifle. He hurried through the cold for four miles to the Hegland cabin, kicked the door, and burst in with the .223 spraying bullets. Les owned several weapons but got no chance to reach one. Les, Flo, and Maxine all fell dying to the cabin floor. Hastings gave each a final bullet in the back of the head.

Hastings realized he would have to hide the bodies. He was counting on others coming to the cabin and wanted to shoot them on arrival, not have them frightened away by the dead. He dragged their bodies one by one to a rear bedroom and stacked them neatly on top of each other. The cabin's outside door hung by a hinge and Hastings' clothes and the kitchen floor were bloodied, but the trap would have to do.

Bleeding and terrified, Chris Richards ran breathlessly, trying but failing to lace up his flopping boots. When he arrived outside the Nash cabin, he called for help. Tim Nash rushed out and asked Richards how he had cut his eye.

"Goddamn it, I've been shot," he answered. "Lou shot me." Thinking Hastings was right behind him, Richards added: "As soon as you see him, start blasting."

Young Nash assumed Richards and Hastings had been fighting and urged him to relax. Nash saw nobody on the trail behind Richards and assumed the incident was probably over. But Richards was adamant. "I'll calm down when you load all your guns," he said.

Nash and his bride gave Richards first aid, then put him on their snowmachine and headed for the airport. There they found pilot Gary Greene working on his airplane. Greene offered to fly Richards to the hospital at Glennallen. While the pilot broke off his mechanical work and loaded Richards into the plane, Tim Nash ran to warn the Heglands that Lou Hastings had apparently run amok. He arrived at the Hegland cabin to find the door hanging off and the scent of gunsmoke in the air. He entered carefully, shotgun at the ready, and found the three bodies stacked in the bedroom. As Nash turned to leave, Hastings emerged from hiding and shot him in the leg with the .223. Nash countered with a shotgun blast, lightly wounding Hastings.

Nash then ran limping back to the airfield and urged his wife Amy to climb into Greene's plane with Richards, but she refused. She would not leave her new husband and felt they should both stay to wave off Lynn Ellis, who would soon be inbound with the mail.

As Greene's plane climbed away from the tiny airstrip, Hastings circled behind Tim and Amy, killing them both from hiding. He approached, shot them again in the head, and dragged their bodies down the runway. He tried to hide the bodies behind a snow berm to avoid alerting pilot Lynn Ellis and anyone coming to meet him.

Harley King was then approaching the airstrip on his snowmachine, with Donna Byram standing on the runners of the dogsled trailing behind. Donna noticed blood on the snow and wondered which of her neighbors might be shooting and skinning animals so close to the runway. She looked up to see the newly-weds' bodies lying on a berm and Hastings standing beside them, raising the .223 rifle and pointing it toward her and Harley.

Donna watched horrified as a line of bullets spattered across the snow toward them, each kicking up a plume of white. Donna could hear nothing because of the snowmachine's engine noise, nor could Harley. She lurched when a bullet slammed into her shoulder, causing Harley to look back at her. He was immediately struck in the back by a bullet, and then more bullets bounced off the new Ski-Doo, which veered into a snowbank and overturned.

Donna tried to help Harley back onto the snowmachine, but couldn't move him. Hastings was jogging toward them. "Harley," she said, "he's going to kill us." King answered, "Yes he is, kid." Then Harley had a thought and grinned weakly. "Now look, both of us don't need to die. Go up and see if Les has a gun. I'll distract him."

Donna ran in terror into the nearby trees. Hastings started to pursue her but stopped when Harley called to him. "Here I am," Harley yelled, "over this way." Hastings ran to Harley King and put two bullets into the back of his head, then ran after Donna.

Still running furiously, Donna saw the kicked-in door at the Heglands and went past. She hid behind the Hegland greenhouse and listened while Hastings stomped up from the runway. Crouching in fear, she remembered something Harley had told her long before about how astute hunters found their quarry. "It's always the movement that attracts the hunter's eye," he had said. She froze and waited.

Hastings searched the house and peered inside the greenhouse. From behind it, Donna heard him muttering: "One not dead, one not dead." She huddled in fear, wishing she had brought the pistol she usually carried as protection from animals. But she had left it at home today, knowing Harley would protect her from danger.

Mail pilot Lynn Ellis was approaching McCarthy when he passed Greene's outgoing plane. Greene radioed Ellis, warning against landing, saying Louis Hastings had gone berserk and was killing people. Ellis called his base and asked the radio operator to alert State Troopers. Then he headed back to Glennallen.

Troopers called Alyeska Pipeline Service Company, operators of the trans-Alaska pipeline, and requested the emergency loan of a helicopter to carry a response team to McCarthy. Within minutes the chopper and three armed officers were en route with a pilot to the scene of the massacre. But the slow-moving helicopter took an hour and a half to reach the village.

Finding nobody left to kill, Hastings tied two duffel bags loaded with weapons, ammunition, and survival gear onto a snowmachine and headed into the wilderness. The troopers from the helicopter found the bodies at the airstrip and inside the Hegland cabin, and the charred ruins of Kennecott Lodge. They searched the area for Hastings and any survivors, but found nobody alive, then returned to the helicopter. They took off, circled the community, and spotted snowmachine tracks heading into the mountains.

The chopper pulled overhead about 2:00 p.m. and the man driving the snowmachine waved to them. The troopers landed nearby and cautiously approached the man on the idling snowmachine. The blood-soaked driver told them he was Chris Richards and was one of the few survivors from McCarthy. He said his neighbor Louis Hastings had flipped his lid and was shooting everybody in the village. He had been lucky to escape and was racing to get help.

The troopers knew the real Chris Richards was then being treated for his wounds at the Glennallen hospital. When it became apparent they knew who Hastings was and were about to arrest him, he said. "Well, I'm your man."

Troopers confiscated the .223 rifle that Hastings carried. It was a Ruger Mini-14 wrapped with black electrical tape; its stock and front sight had been removed, giving it the appearance of a commando weapon. Hastings carried several hundred rounds of ammunition in clips and packets. In his duffel bags they found a police radio scanner, smokeless rifle powder, wire cutters, flares, a small flare gun, a large hunting knife, and a knife sharpener. One bag contained a black homemade stocking cap, an all-black set of clothing, and a coded computer printout containing the names of the two hundred prominent Alaskans and police officers. The officers loaded Hastings into the helicopter, lifted off, and headed back to McCarthy, leaving the duffel bags and snowmachine to be retrieved later.

The troopers found Donna Byram still crouching in hiding behind the greenhouse, nearly hysteri-
cal from the cold and loss of blood. For a time she
refused to believe they were troopers and thought the
helicopter was part of the murder plot. Later, in the
Hegland cabin, they found a silencer wrapped in a
bloody beaver pelt, which Hastings had apparently
dropped, and in his cabin was a pistol rigged so it
could be concealed in a sleeve and fired by pulling a
string.

Earlier that morning when Bonnie Morris returned home from the Heglands' house, she had gone
about her chores and listened for the sound of the
mail plane's engine. Maxine Edwards never showed
up for her cookies, but Bonnie assumed Maxine had
been too busy and gone straight home. She heard a
few shots, but those were nothing unusual around
McCarthy, where everyone had guns and often prac-
ticed shooting.

At noon she listened to Caribou Clatter, a radio show
on KCAM, Glennallen, that broadcast personal messages
for residents of the area's isolated bush communities.
The program included an unusual message from Ellis
Air Taxi saying the mail plane wouldn't be coming.
Bonnie went into the woods with her friend Malcolm
Vance to cut logs, then listened to the news that evening.
Horrified, she heard that six people had been killed in
McCarthy. She hurriedly switched to an Anchorage sta-
tion; the report was the same.

"Six people," she said. "That was just about everyone we could think of." Shortly afterward they heard a
helicopter circling overhead, saw it shining a search-
light down into the surrounding trees. "We thought there

was somebody still out there in the woods. We huddled under the bed. Finally the troopers found us. We were the only light, the only surviving couple in town."

Hastings was tried the following year for six murders and two attempted murders; he was convicted and sentenced to 634 years in prison. The judge called him an environmental terrorist, a man who sought to portray himself as the savior of Alaska, preserver of the wilderness. Hastings later appealed the sentence, saying he had been rendered temporarily insane by inhaling heavy doses of organic copper while applying preservative log oil at his cabin. The appeal went nowhere.

Bonnie Morris was devastated by the murders. As troopers were still loading her friends' bodies into the helicopter, she told a newspaper reporter: "These are the people who inspired the rest of us when we came here to build a sane and healthy life. A nobody came in here and wiped out the pillars of one of the few self-sufficient communities in Alaska."

Jo King buried her husband Harley under a tree at Long Lake, a place he had told Jo was his favorite spot in the world.

INDEX

ABOUT THE ILLUSTRATOR

BRIAN SOSTROM studied art at Washington State University where he received a BFA. After graduation he continued pursuing both illustration and fine art. He has spent much of his professional career creating and designing artwork for video games. In 1997 he co founded a Seattle area game development company where he is currently collaborating with other artists. Brian spends much of his spare time painting and pursuing outdoor interests.

ABOUT THE AUTHOR

TOM BRENNAN is a newspaper editor, columnist and business consultant based in Anchorage. Born in Massachusetts, he and his wife Marnie quit their jobs at a New England newspaper in 1967 and drove cross-country while towing a houseboat on wheels. It was a six-week journey that convinced them they didn't want to drive it both ways. In Anchorage, Tom became a reporter for *The Anchorage Times*, then worked for many years in the oil industry both as an in-house executive and external consultant. He became a writer for the *The Voice of The Anchorage Times* in 2000.

RECOMMENDATIONS FOR READERS
interested in Alaska and its people:

ARCTIC BUSH PILOT: A Memoir, by James "Andy" Anderson
as told to Jim Rearden, trade paperback, $16.95

COLD RIVER SPIRITS: The Legacy of an Athabascan-Irish Family
from Alaska's Yukon River, by Jan Harper-Haines, hardbound, $19.95

COLD STARRY NIGHT: An Alaska Memoir, by Claire Fejes,
trade paperback, $19.95

FASHION MEANS YOUR FUR HAT IS DEAD: A Guide to Good
Manners & Social Survival in Alaska, by Mike Doogan, trade
paperback, $14.95

FATHER OF THE IDITAROD: The Joe Redington Story,
by Lew Freedman, trade paperback, $16.95

JIM REARDEN'S ALASKA: Fifty Years of Frontier Adventure,
by Jim Rearden, trade paperback, $17.95

MOMENTS RIGHTLY PLACED: An Aleutian Memoir,
by Ray Hudson, trade paperback, $14.95

OUR ALASKA: Personal Stories about Life in Alaska,
edited by Mike Doogan, trade paperback, $14.95

RIDING THE WILD SIDE OF DENALI, by Miki & Julie Collins,
trade paperback, $14.95

TALES OF ALASKA'S BUSH RAT GOVERNOR: The Extraordinary
Autobiography of Jay Hammond, Wilderness Guide and Reluctant
Politician, trade paperback, $17.95

EPICENTER PRESS / *Alaska Book Adventures*